TEACHER WORK

How to Ma
Get Your Li

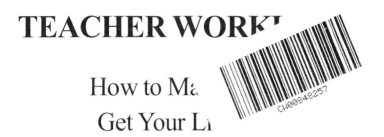

Bruno Gomes

Cover illustration Copyright © www.depositphotos.com
Cover design by pixelstudio https://www.fiverr.com/pixelstudio
Editing and proofreading by KN Editorial https://kneditorial.com/
Formatting by around86 https://www.fiverr.com/around86
ISBN: 9798617224810
Get in touch with the author bruno@teacherworkload.com

<u>Acknowledgements</u>

I would like to publicly thank all the teachers, support staff, senior leaders and students who I have worked with throughout the years. Thank you to my wonderful and supportive wife, as well as my family. Thank you to everyone who offered kind words of encouragement throughout this process. Thank you to the launch team – you made it possible to turn a post-it mind map into a published book. I am hugely grateful.

Launch team members

Leanne

Vikkie

Karen

Nageen

Sophie

Kirstyn

Dan

Amy

Emily

Pam

Contents

1. The root of the issue

The vast majority of teachers enjoy teaching and are positive about their workplace and colleagues, but they are disappointed by the profession. According to the UK's Health and Safety Executive, teaching staff and education professionals report the highest rates of work-related stress, depression and anxiety in Britain.

True account

It's the 22nd of August and the GCSE results are out. I exchange the usual text messages with my closest teacher friends about how our classes have performed. Charlotte feels bad because her grades are not all in line with targets set by the school for her students. She feels that 'she hasn't invested as much time as she could', because most days, she was leaving school by 5:30pm. She doesn't want to be an 'average' teacher.

I worked with Charlotte for a number of years at a previous school, and she's a phenomenal teacher, well above average. She is the kind of professional that our young people need and deserve in the classroom. We don't want her to leave the profession, just like thousands of burnt out teachers who quit, or plan to quit, every year.

Teaching doesn't have to be like this:

"I spend every evening and weekend working. If I don't, I feel guilty for not working and I am made to feel guilty as well.

I am now planning to leave the profession - the workload is making me ill and I want my life back."

"I find it hard to make time for family and friends - and when I do, I find it increasingly stressful worrying about what I am not doing for work."

"I'm not able to have a life. I hate this job. Nothing is ever good enough. It's not about the children, it's about data."

"It's unmanageable and I need a new career. I'm unhappy most of the time and am unwell with stress and anxiety. It affects my family time considerably - I often miss time with my children and when I do spend time with them it's not quality as I'm either too tired or am worrying about what I have to do."

These quotes from a survey report by the National Education Union on teacher workload in schools and academies make for depressing reading. A colossal 81% of teachers surveyed said that they have considered leaving teaching in the last year because of workload. I've been there myself, and I have come out of the other end triumphant.

In this book I'm going to show you that it is possible to be a guilt-free, effective teacher, without compromising on the quality of your teaching or time with friends and family, and without giving away your precious evenings, weekends and holidays.

The book includes true and tested strategies which continue to work well for me, and I'm confident they will work for you. I'll provide you with 'real world' tools from someone who, just like you, is in the classroom Monday to Friday. It's not a collection of educational blog entries with insipid advice and it's not an attempt to refer you to other books for further reading and guidance.

I'm going to demonstrate how you can tackle your ever-increasing workload, including both ways of reducing it and ways to improve your own productivity. I'm going to show you that it is possible to obtain healthy levels of occupational well-being and truly achieve a work-life balance. You are going to get your life back.

2. <u>The mindset</u>

My 'wake-up call' moment

I'd been teaching for five years and had just got a job at a new school as Teacher in Charge of Spanish. This was at an inner London mixed comprehensive academy which pushed me to my limits. The school day was long with six one-hour periods, and there were constant after-school meetings and events, daily morning briefings and an absurd amount of activities not directly related to teaching. I'm not one to shy away from hard work, so I got stuck in.

And it completely and utterly took over my life. I worked late evenings and pretty much whole weekends. I caught up on work during the holidays. Towards the end of the academic year, my body couldn't handle it any longer and I got shingles. This was due to the physical and emotional exertion I'd submitted myself to; the chemicals released by my body in reaction to my stress levels being through the roof prevented my immune system from working properly. I was bedridden in pain for a week.

Still, I didn't change my ways. For the next couple of years, I carried on in this zombie-like state of incessant work. But then my mind started to play tricks on me. I'm a keen sportsperson and cycle to and from work on a daily basis. I started to develop thoughts along the lines of "if only I could fall off my bike and hurt myself, I wouldn't have to go to school". The thoughts got darker over time, and just were not going away. It was clear that not only my physical health but also my mental health was suffering, and immediate action needed to be taken. So I did, before my job literally killed me.

Important: I never spoke to anyone about this. Fortunately, I was able to gather strength through my family and pull myself together. If you have or are experiencing similar issues, please do speak to someone. You are not alone in your fight.

Now, I never work evenings, and unless I have a meeting, I leave school at 4:30pm – sometimes even earlier. I don't work on the weekends and rarely do any work during the holidays. I go to the gym Monday to Friday. I spend quality time with my family, especially my wife and two-year-old son. This has had no negative impact whatsoever in my effectiveness as a teacher and the learning of my students. In fact, quite the opposite. I'm better in the classroom. I'm more alert, I'm more energetic and I can therefore deliver better lessons to the young people in front of me.

The Department for Education's 2016 Teacher Workload Survey showed that classroom teachers spent, on average, 55.4 hours a week on teaching and other teaching-related work. 25% of respondents reported working more than 60 hours a week. For the 2019/20 academic year, if you're a Newly Qualified Teacher outside of the London area with a 7.4% pension contribution, those 60 hours equate to a take home pay of just under £6 an hour. If you're working at the lower end of the average – 48 hours a week – and you're on the upper pay range 3 with a pension contribution of 9.6%, you're pocketing £11.20 an hour.

So obviously, we don't do it for the money. We do it because every day we make a difference to our students' lives. We do it because we're passionate about our subjects and we want to share that knowledge.

Nevertheless, have you looked at your pension statement lately? Mine says 'retirement age: 67 years and 3 months'. Most teachers I know say there's no way they can work, or will work, until that age. The hard truth of the matter, however, is that you may well have to work into your late sixties, or even beyond. And although the very limited data available suggests that it's an 'urban myth' that teachers tend to die within a few years of retirement, I'm not so sure. In 15 years of teaching, I've only worked with two colleagues who retired after working in the same department as me. Both of them encountered this tragic fate. I certainly don't intend find out the hard way myself.

How do you protect yourself from this stressful lifestyle? The answer is that you MUST have a plan. And the plan must attach substantially greater value to your most precious asset – TIME. The plan is to live continuously, not just during (part of) the holidays. The plan is to strive for a work-life balance, not to start enjoying life when you retire. The plan is to work efficiently, and still be a great teacher without compromising on your personal life.

You know that the pace at which you're currently working is unsustainable. Research commissioned by the Department for Education in 2019 shows that 76% of secondary teachers and 70% of primary teachers say their workload is unachievable within their contracted hours. Let's make it so. What would happen if you really couldn't work evenings, weekends or holidays? Say you were a carer for someone else, for example. What happens when you have a medical appointment and have to leave by a certain (much earlier than usual) time? What happens on a partner's birthday, or on your own birthday?

What happens is that you make sure that what needs to be done gets done. You become focused and prioritise accordingly. You eliminate menial jobs and target those that will have the biggest impact on your workload. And you leave with a sense of accomplishment, or you simply postpone some obligations until the next working day.

The main issue with teachers' workload is not what you think it is. It's not that you simply have too much to do. It is, in fact, the contrary – you have TOO much time to do it in. You work in a job which allows you to carry out tasks anywhere. You can do some marking on a plane, some planning on the sofa, or check your emails after dinner.

Parkinson's law (coined by British naval historian and author Cyril Northcote Parkinson in 1957) states that "work expands so as to fill the time available for its completion". In other words, the longer you give yourself to accomplish a task, the longer it will take – and as teachers, any time of the day is potential working time. You could ALWAYS do a bit more, and you've allowed yourself to do so.

So, first and foremost, you have to change your mindset. School work is to be accomplished at school. Full stop. You're going to reduce the time you give yourself to execute tasks and, in doing so, you will reduce the time it takes to get them done. It's a bit like packing a suitcase to go on holiday. The bigger the suitcase, the more you'll pack into it, even though you know you won't use most of the items you add.

YOU WILL NOT engage in **'hollow'** work: Time-consuming, logistical-style tasks, often performed while distracted, which do not create new value – e.g. checking your email.

YOU WILL engage in **'engrossed'** work: professional activities performed in a state of distraction-free concentration that push your cognitive abilities to excel – e.g. lesson planning.

In turn, YOU WILL achieve an authentic work-life balance.

Key takeaways

- The demanding nature of a teaching job can lead to physical and mental health concerns. These must be tackled with decisive action.
- It is possible to leave school at a reasonable time, not work evenings or weekends, and nonetheless be an effective teacher.
- You must have a work-life balance plan for your career.
- A teacher's job always allows for tasks to be completed away from school, which can lead to inefficient use of time.
- The longer you give yourself to complete an obligation, the longer it will take.

- You must engage more in 'engrossed' work and less in 'hollow' work.

3. **Technology vs time**

Teachers know all too well that technology often fails us. You have a lesson observation and the interactive whiteboard won't switch on. You found a really useful YouTube video for your challenging Year 8 class on Thursday afternoon and the sound doesn't work. Ofsted is in and you can't access your lessons on the shared drive because the internet is down. You send a kid running to IT support, but they come back with a confused look: "They said you have to send an email and raise a *ticket…*".

But that's not even what I'm talking about. Technology is now failing teachers on a much greater scale. We spend so much time with it and have become so reliant on it that it is now hindering us more than it is helping us. It is impoverishing as much as it is enriching. Constant interruptions and distractions, even if short, delay the total time required to complete a task. They're killing your productivity and your ability to perform activities well. So let's see where time can be saved, and efficiency can be maximised, by avoiding technology.

Smartphones

64% of people in the UK claim that their mobile distracts them at work. Smartphones are checked on average once every 12 minutes. You probably use your mobile phone at work for personal reasons. We all do. But that's not what's destroying our productivity. What's doing the most damage is the constant interruptions and distractions.

There is quite simply no way we can make the most of our workday when we can't work uninterrupted for a set period of time. People who get interrupted when they're in the middle of a task can take up to 35 minutes to bring their focus back to it. Where on earth do we as teachers have 35 minutes to spare? On a good day, you might just about be able to finish a cup of tea without it getting cold.

If you really want to achieve the holy grail of work-life balance, this is a great place to start. If you are 'brave' enough, simply leave your phone at home. You've immediately won the battle and increased your daily output. If that's not an option for you, for whatever reason, as soon as you get to work – or even before – switch it off. The least you can do is put it on airplane mode and keep out of sight. Still can't bring yourself to do it? Turn off all notifications, including group chat ones. Over time, you'll feel the need to check your phone less and less.

If you still can't resist having the odd peek, then try creating an inconvenience. Keep your phone as far away from you as possible, such as in another room. You'll still be able to access it when you need it, but just the hassle of having to go and get it will be enough to reduce the amount that you use it at work.

My final piece of advice on mobile phones relates to your sanity more than it does to being efficient with time. Do not send or reply to work-related text messages. I was once on holiday in August and, after a night out, I got an early morning text from my then Head of Department. It went on to tell me that she had sent me an email and listed some tasks that she needed me to do before we got back to work a week later. This put a dampener on the rest of my holiday as I now had those work matters hanging over me for the week. It made me feel so bad that I decided never to send a work-related text message to someone in my team on a personal device – and I never have. Work should not be allowed to blend into your personal life.

Email

According to research data gathered through the Teacher Tapp app, teachers are spending six hours a week answering emails.

The reason we spend so much time on email is because we are constantly checking it, and these small chunks of time soon start to add up. And even in these small chunks, email makes us less productive because, similarly to phones, it interrupts the natural flow of work.

I absolutely understand why we do it. There's a feeling of instant gratification when we get an email – even if we complain we get too many of them – so we feel the need to have a look often. Checking our emails is also something which is 'easy' to do, as it requires very little effort, so we tend to find it more attractive than longer, more complex tasks like marking that set of books. But there's more: if you're constantly reading and replying to emails you are 'visibly' busy. In other words, you're convincing yourself and others that you're doing your job well.

There are clearly gargantuan opportunities here for time savings and a productivity boost. So, let's start with the basics.

If you access your school email on your smartphone, disable it now. Just stop reading and do it.

True account

I created some tracking spreadsheets for the new GCSE languages specification and emailed it to colleagues at my previous school, including the line manager for Modern Foreign Languages. Demi replied a couple of weeks later, saying she missed that email but thank you for sharing. Her email was sent at 1:15am. She had been attending to her two-year-old daughter who had woken her up, but she couldn't help checking her phone and answering a few work emails.

This is an extreme example, but it's not at all uncommon for teachers to be working on email long into the night. Stop now, and instead take a more focused approach. Do not check, reply or send emails in the evening, on weekends or during holidays.

I learned this the hard way. I used to have my work email on my phone and at times it ruined my evenings, because of some tetchy message or some admin task I hadn't yet done. Once, having checked my email on my phone immediately after waking up, I replied to an email about whether or not I would be striking the following week. The trouble was that in my half-asleep state, I 'replied all' and thus informed the whole school. Not fun. No chance of it ever happening again though, since work emails on my personal devices are now a thing of the past.

Never check your email in the morning. If you do, you're immediately putting other people's priorities ahead of yours.

True account

Lately Jessica has had some disagreements with her Head of Year. She's being asked to undertake some pastoral tasks which are just unreasonable on a full-time teaching timetable. This is causing some friction between the two and raising Jessica's stress levels. It's Friday, and Jessica teaches periods 2 all the way to 6, finishing off with a double period with a challenging Year 11 group.

Jessica checks her email and finds that she's been asked to attend a meeting period 1 with the Head of Year and a member of the leadership team regarding her pastoral obligations. I intervene and tell them that this is not a 'free' period but a time for planning and preparation. The meeting doesn't take place, but the damage is done. Jessica is now anxious and worried. This has a negative impact on the five lessons she now has to teach.

This is called attention 'residue'. When you switch from one task to another your attention does not immediately follow and 'residue' of your attention remains stuck on the previous task, which will in turn result in poor performance in your next activity. The more intense the 'residue', the worse the performance. This is particularly true of attention 'residue' relating to email, especially if it is something that you can't immediately action.

Only check your email once a day, or not at all. If you have to check it, do so after school and only if you've accomplished all of your own work first. The minute you look at your inbox, you will be doing other people's work. It will be full of emails asking you to do things you don't want or plan to do, and presenting you with problems that you now have to deal with.

At the busiest of times, I will go three or four days without checking my emails – even as a Head of Department. When I do go through them, I do so in one quick, continuous stretch. You won't miss out on any vital information. Whatever you can't action there and then, make a note of it in your daily plan (more on that later – you will be using the good old pen and paper a lot more to master your workload).

If an email is that important people will come and find you to talk about it and the same is true even if it's not. How many times have you had someone approach you and start a conversation with "I've sent you an email ..." which they then proceed to tell you all about? Besides, everything you need to know is in the calendar, was mentioned in morning briefings and after school meetings, and was written in the previous week's bulletin. No need to worry. The worst that can happen is that the sender has to wait three or four days for a reply. Not the end of the world.

If you have to send an email, take a similar approach. Only send it in your email checking time – after school, once, never in the mornings. If you can't do it at this time, just pick up a phone or go and find the person. Avoid sending the email in the first place; the more emails you send the more emails you'll get.

It's substantially more effective – people speak much more quickly than they type and can express themselves better too. It avoids someone misinterpreting what you're trying to communicate. An eight or ten-email thread over several days with lots of people carbon copied in can be a simple five or ten-minute conversation.

Let's take the example of the dreaded 'Can we meet at some point this week?' email. If it's not possible to apply the strategy above and speak in person to the sender, then invest a bit more time composing a message that prevents the exchange from spiralling into something longer than a Year 10 Snapchat streak.

This might seem like conflicting advice – spending more time writing an email to spend less time on your email – but it saves you precious minutes (or hours) reading and responding to other messages in the long run. For instance, in response to the email requesting a meeting, your reply should look something like this:

Hi Michael, I can meet with you this week in my classroom GF15 on Monday at 8am, Tuesday or Wednesday at 3:30pm or Thursday at 12:20pm. If none of these times suit you, there is no need to reply to this email. Call me in the MFL workroom or see me just after morning briefing on Wednesday. We can arrange a suitable time then. Thank you.

This email warrants just one possible email response confirming a suitable meeting time for the receiver. All of the other scenarios don't require a response at all. It 'closes the loop' and prevents any further unnecessary messages.

Do not feel that you have to respond to every email you get, even if it's just to thank someone. Teachers overthink the importance of replying to emails because the sender assumes they will get a reply, even when one isn't needed.

In one of the schools I worked at, there was a member of the leadership team who everyone respected as far as her ability to conduct her role. However, she frustrated a lot of people by not responding enough to her emails. Guess what? We all survived and quickly adjusted, finding other ways to solve the matters in question, without the need to congest her inbox. Once you get past the discomfort of this approach, and others stop expecting your responses to their emails, you will begin to reap its rewards.

One issue you might come across is when there is a crucial piece of information in an email you were sent, which you need to retrieve in order to continue making progress on your current task. I found myself in a similar situation recently. I gave in to temptation and couldn't help going into my email, even though it wasn't my dedicated email checking time. But of course I didn't stop at the information I needed, and I couldn't avoid glancing at all the other 'urgent' new messages. Thirty minutes later and with several emails read and replied to, I couldn't even remember what information I went in to look for in the first place. So, you must RESIST the temptation! If you end up stuck, just move on to your next planned task and wait until it's your official email checking time.

"But Bruno, I must check my email regularly because (insert excuse here) …". You don't. Checking your email is 'hollow' work and it's killing your productivity. You are a teacher, not a desk worker.

True account

Eleanor has not long ago been appointed as a new Deputy Head of Year 8. She's keen to get involved straight away with the year team and the emails start flowing. I'm on the receiving end of many of these, but most do not actually apply to me. I come across Eleanor while on duty and challenge her over it. I ask her not to send them to me in the first place. She tells me, "Just delete them".

Her heart is in the right place, but let's just look at this seemingly harmless statement. Conservatively, teachers receive six emails a day which are not directly addressed to them (carbon copied or otherwise). They've landed in your inbox, so you still read them, if only to determine whether they contain anything relevant for you. If it takes you just one minute for each email, that equates to 30 minutes a week. Over an academic year, we're talking 19.5 hours just deleting emails! This is just the tip of the iceberg. I reinforced my point to Eleanor and continue to do so with colleagues when emails get too frivolous.

Key takeaways

- Technology is failing teachers due to the constant interruptions to our workflow.

- Turn off all notifications on your smartphone.
- Leave your phone at home, put it on airplane mode, or create an 'inconvenience' to keep you away from it.
- Disable your work email on your smartphone.
- Don't check your email outside of working hours.
- Don't check your emails in the morning.
- Only check your email once you've done all your own work.
- Even if you go several days without checking your email, you won't miss out on any important information.
- Don't respond to every email; not all of them warrant a reply.
- Avoid sending emails in the first place and instead speak to people over the phone or in person.
- Write concise emails which 'close the loop'.
- Ask others to stop sending you emails which are not directly meant for you.

4. <u>Your school day</u>

Good habits

We are creatures of habit, and you may well be stuck in some bad ones when it comes to managing your workload. Create some new, healthier, and more powerful habits.

Start your day an hour earlier. Not a morning person? Neither was I, but needs must. Try it for two weeks until it becomes second nature, and you won't even remember how hard it might have been to start off with. **Side note**: aim for a minimum of five 90-minute sleep cycles; set your alarm to wake you up in 7 hours and 40 minutes, which allows for ten minutes to fall asleep. Need more sleep? Go for 6 cycles – 9 hours and 10 minutes.

The benefits of getting out of bed earlier will be unequivocal. Firstly, you'll save time on your commute by avoiding rush hour, especially if you're driving. The world is still asleep, so when you get to school you can immerse yourself in quiet, uninterrupted – and therefore more productive – work. The minute students and staff start coming in, the noise and distractions start and your performance suffers.

Your brain will have had all night to rest so your concentration will be enhanced. As a teacher, your school day consists of a barrage of stimulus and decision-making. Each decision leads to 'decision fatigue' and a decrease in willpower strength (the ability to resist distractions), which consequently clouds your mind.

Once you're at school, there'll be fewer interruptions from co-workers and yes, the photocopier will be free.

Do you have commitments which simply don't allow you to get to school early, like dropping children off at nursery? Find another way. Perhaps a partner can help on certain days, or you get up an hour earlier anyway and do an hour's productive work while everyone is asleep. Make something work for your circumstances.

Important: Don't loaf. If you're going to get up earlier and maximise this strategy, don't allow yourself to think 'I've got plenty of time'. In order to really reap the benefits, instil a sense of urgency in your morning routine.

Come in with a plan – and stick to it

This is probably the most important section of this book. If you take nothing else from it, understand the importance of planning your school day in order to maximise your daily output and be efficient with your time. You wouldn't go into a lesson without some sort of plan, and the same approach must be taken when tackling your day. You must always know what you'll be doing before school, during your non-contact periods and after school.

The teaching profession is not naturally conducive to effective, productive work. You are obliged to work in chunks – a free period here and there – so having a plan before you start your day is crucial. This needs to be done on pen and paper, whether in your planner or on a sticky note. Stay away from technology. It doesn't have to be anything fancy or too detailed, just enough to set you on a productive path for the day. Here's an example:

- Before school: plan Year 8 and Year 10 lessons for tomorrow
- Teach periods 1 and 2
- Non-contact period 3: continue planning Year 8 and 10 lessons (if not finished) mark twelve Year 11 exercise books
- Teach period 4 and 5
- After school – go to front gate duty
- Finish marking Year 11 books (if not finished)
- Photocopy resources for tomorrow's lessons
- Periphery tasks:
    - see colleague X about resources for Year 9
    - call parent of student Y
    - complete UCAS Year 13 predictions on SIMS
- Unforeseen tasks (add here)
- Check email
- Draft tomorrow's plan

Notice that lesson planning is at the top of this plan, quickly followed by marking. These are more mentally demanding tasks and form the fundamental principles of teaching, since they determine the fate of your career. If your delivery in the classroom is exceptional and the feedback (written or otherwise) you give to students matches it, everything else comes together. They ought to be your priority. For example, I know that I'm not a great pastoral tutor. I'm aware I could be much more effective, but the reality of the teaching profession is that I'm just not given the appropriate time to do it, upsetting as that is. So, I either allow myself to be an ordinary tutor but an excellent teacher or vice-versa. I chose the former, as teaching is my main role and it's where I add more value. Now, you might argue here that you can be outstanding at both, and I would agree. However, when you add up all the other teaching obligations that the job entails, at some point you can only be ordinary at some things. Either that, or you'll burn out and then you're no good to anyone. You can't be superb at everything. Simply allow yourself to be 'enough' at some small things so you can be brilliant at the big things.

One issue you might encounter, particularly if you are new to scheduling your day with a plan, is that at first you're likely to underestimate the time you require for most tasks. Start with conservative estimates and allow for 'if not finished' bullet points, as in the example above. Over time, you'll become more accurate at predicting how long different tasks will take.

Email should always be the penultimate task on your plan. As mentioned in the previous chapter, you should work for yourself first and then for others – which is what happens when you look at your inbox. If you haven't accomplished everything else in your plan, or it is simply time to go home, skip email checking for the day.

The very last job before you leave is drafting a plan for your next working day. This will allow you to truly reap the benefits of downtime. More on that below.

Important: Do NOT deviate from your plan. You know what it's like; no two days are the same, so there will naturally be obstacles put in your way that will attempt to steer you in an altogether different direction. Some kid was rude to you at break and now you're faced with a lengthy follow up, or a colleague asks you to send them that worksheet you created for Year 7, etc. etc. etc.

Just add these things that crop up during the day to the 'unforeseen tasks' section of your plan and only action them then, NEVER before your daily plan is successfully accomplished.

The only exception to this is a safeguarding matter – this overrules the laws of your plan.

Another essential aspect of your daily plan is to have a clear cut-off point. I get up at 5:00am, so for me it's 4:30pm. I stick rigorously to my daily plan and ensure that I prioritise tasks accordingly, eliminating 'hollow' work in favour of 'engrossed' work. I have clear strategies, which I lay out for you throughout this book. I don't work less than I used to when I worked late evenings and weekends all the time, but I'm significantly more efficient with my time management. I'm much more productive.

Examples of why this approach is effective can be found in totally unrelated industries, for example, in situations where reducing the length of the working week boosts productivity. When Microsoft Japan tested a four-day week, productivity at work shot up by about 40%. One Melbourne organisation found a six-hour working day forced employees to eliminate unproductive activities such as sending pointless emails, sitting in lengthy meetings and 'cyberloafing' (messing around on the internet). British businesses that have successfully switched to a four-day week include Elektra Lighting, Think Productive and Portcullis Legals. Employees were not made to work longer hours each day to make up for the shorter week, they just adapted and worked smarter.

The same will happen to you when you stick to your plan, have a clear cut-off point to your workday, and don't allow yourself to do any schoolwork at home. You give yourself no alternative but to be more efficient and productive. You'll notice that the stuff that always seems so urgent in the moment is actually superfluous.

Engrossed work

Next time you're in your department's workroom, or any other school office, I want you to try to notice something. How conducive are these areas to 'engrossed' work? When teachers arrive in the morning there are conversations about their previous evening or weekends; during your free period someone tells you all about their Year 11 class that just doesn't seem to grasp the fact that their exam is in a few months' time, and they really need to apply themselves more; it's the end of the school day and there are phone calls being made to parents, as well as a personal one to book a medical appointment.

The point I am trying to make is that these open plan workspaces prevent us from reaching optimum productivity levels. It's just human nature. Your instinctive desire to get involved in what's happening around you will win over your willpower to get your work done. As the day goes on and your brain tires, the harder it is to resist these distractions.

J.K. Rowling booked herself into a room at the Balmoral Hotel in Edinburgh to finish writing The Deathly Hallows, even though she had no intention of actually staying there. Peter Shankman, an American entrepreneur and author, bought a $4000 return flight to Tokyo in order to write a book and meet a two-week deadline. On the way there, he wrote. When he got to Japan, he got off the plane, stretched his legs, and drank an espresso. Then, he turned right back around and boarded his returning flight back home. And he wrote again. Start to finish, his entire trip lasted less than 30 hours, but he now had a manuscript in hand.

You don't have to go to such extremes. The solution is as simple as finding an empty classroom or another space where you can work uninterrupted. This is especially vital when lesson planning. If you have your own classroom, this might be straightforward, provided someone else doesn't teach there too. If you don't have that luxury, just look up the free classrooms timetable on your school's management information system, or ask the office manager to print it for you. Alternatively, you can simply walk around during your free periods and check for yourself. Once you've figured out where you are going to be working in the morning, during the school day and after school, write it on a printed copy of your timetable and keep it in a visible, easy to reach area.

It's particularly important to have a dedicated isolated workspace during the school day when there are so many people around and therefore a much higher chance of interruptions. Just make sure that before you start working, you have everything you need to do so – a cup of tea, mark schemes, textbooks, resources, etc. – so that you're able to engage in deep concentration and productive work. Do NOT take other unnecessary electronic devices with you, such as your smartphone.

Finding an empty classroom to work in before and after school should not be difficult, but if there just isn't one on a particular free period and you have to work in an open space with colleagues, then try this: put a pair of earplugs or headphones in, and zone out the background noise.

Don't be apprehensive that colleagues might consider this strategy as anti-social or odd. The message you are sending is that you are trying to focus on your work. The message is that you've had enough of working late evenings and weekends, and you want to leave school at a reasonable time without having to do any work when you get home. The message is that you'd rather socialise with colleagues later in the pub, with that guilt-free beverage. The message is that you WANT your life back.

Collaborative work

You're not suddenly going to become a recluse. The nature of a teaching job makes it impossible – and undesirable – to do without human interaction, so you will still be regularly communicating with teachers, students and other staff. This is where collaborative work can be valuable. At times, working with someone else can push you further and yield better results than if you were working alone. Moderating students' work is an obvious example, as is lesson planning.

If you're going to work collaboratively, you MUST keep in mind the same guidelines as above. Plan what you're going to be working on, find a workspace where interruptions and distractions are minimised, have all the resources you need ready, and stay away from needless mobile phones. Make sure you set these expectations with your partner(s).

Engage in 'engrossed' work as you would when working by yourself.

Downtime

I skim read a fair number of educational articles. Every now and then, one grabs my attention with some insipid advice about a teaching profession pain point, which usually makes me sigh. If only it were that simple. It would be hypocritical for me to just say "don't work after you've left school", when I know that's much easier said than done. The reality of the job makes it very difficult not to mentally replay conversations, not to check your email after dinner, not to do some marking or planning while watching Netflix – just to try to catch up or get ahead.

Any teacher can attest to the fact that there are always incomplete tasks and there is always something else you could be doing. You can NEVER reach a point where all your obligations have been handled. The leftover obligations will inevitably battle for your attention throughout the evening or weekend.

This is where drafting your plan for the next working day becomes indispensable for you to truly reap the benefits of downtime. By outlining a plan for the following day, you are releasing your mind from worrying about unfinished tasks. You now know when these will be tackled, freeing up your brain – as well as your evenings and weekends, for other pursuits.

True account

After I'd worked there for a few years, my school introduced a clocking system. We were told that the reason behind it was to ensure that in a fire emergency, all staff could be quickly accounted for. However, word soon spread among staff that the Senior Leadership Team was rejoicing about the fact that some staff were clocking out later than others. Paul, a Newly Qualified Teacher, worked at school until 8:00 or 9:00pm every day, which was worthy of praise.

It is nearly 6:00pm and Camila, who's also newly qualified, is about to go home. As she's leaving, her Head of Department mentions that when she was at the same stage in her own career, she never left school without taking home a set of exercise books to mark in the evening.

The approach presented in the two examples above, although well-meant, is counter-productive. The aim is clearly to get more out of teachers, but the complete opposite is what actually happens. It would be like a football manager increasing training sessions by two or three hours a day to obtain winning results on matchday. The outcome is the inverse: tired players and losses for the team.

The same happens with teachers. If you are pushed, or push yourself, to exhaustion, you simply can't perform at your best where you add the most value: in the classroom. The human cost is difficult to quantify, but lesson quality inevitably suffers, and overall student progress is hindered. On the other hand, the financial cost of having fatigued teachers who simply can't cope with going into work and have to take time off is easily measured – approximately £1.3 billion spent on supply teaching each year. The message to school leaders is therefore clear-cut; look after your teachers and they will look after the students. In turn, the school budget takes care of itself.

If you ever find yourself working sizeable productive days and that still doesn't seem to be enough for school leaders, point them in the direction of this chapter and the advantages of downtime which I summarise below:

- **The work you do in the evenings is inefficient and unimportant** – You have been at work the whole day, and you've hit your brain's daily concentration capacity. Mental fatigue has taken over and you're likely to only engage in slow-paced minor tasks anyway. You aren't going to be able to plan outstanding lessons or produce high-quality resources. By deferring this work, you aren't missing out on much.

- **Downtime helps with your insights** – Providing your conscious brain with time to rest enables your unconscious mind to take a shift, sorting through your most complex teaching challenges. In other words, if you're not distracted by work-related issues in the evenings and weekends, you will make better decisions and end up performing better.

- **Downtime helps recharge the energy needed to work intensely** – And you know as well as I do that working in a school is astonishingly intense. This seems obvious, but there is scientific evidence to back it up, as studies have shown that you must replenish your finite 'directed attention' resources. If you don't, you'll struggle to concentrate the following working day. Think of your brain as a muscle exercised when weightlifting. If you went to the gym every day and always trained the same muscle group, you would seriously hinder your progress. Muscles need recovery time to function at their best, and so does your brain. Do what works for you, whether it's quality time with a partner, family or friends; listening to music; going for a walk in nature; reading a novel. Now that your evenings are free to enjoy, the sky is the limit.

Important: Don't be tempted to do even a small amount of work after you've gone home. If necessary, extend your workday at school, but when you are done, commit yourself to being done. Even a short interruption to your well-deserved and beneficial downtime can linger for a long time to follow. It is not uncommon to glance at a distressing email in the evening and then have its implications haunt your thoughts and keep you half-awake throughout the night.

Key takeaways

- Create and stick to new powerful work habits.
- Start your day an hour earlier and reap its benefits.
- If getting up earlier is not possible for you, commit to other morning changes which do work for you.
- Apply a sense of urgency to your morning routine.
- Write up a plan of your schedule as it will increase your productivity. This should be drafted the previous working day.
- Lesson planning and marking students' work need to be at the top of your priorities. They are the most important aspects of teaching.
- Accept that you cannot be brilliant at everything that comes with the profession. If you are excellent only at teaching and learning, you are an outstanding professional.
- Allow for extra time to accomplish tasks – be conservative in your time allocation to begin with.
- Email should be the second-to-last job of the working day, time permitting.
- Do not stray from your plan, except for a safeguarding matter.
- Have a clear cut-off point to your working day. This will make you more focused.
- Open plan school offices are not conducive to productive work. It's difficult to ignore distractions which are happening around you, especially as the day goes on.
- Find an empty classroom or a designated empty workspace and accomplish your work there.

- Don't worry about what others might think of your strategies. You will be more effective than most other teachers. You will truly achieve a work-life balance.
- Working collaboratively can at times have greater benefits than working by yourself. However, keep in mind the same rules as for working in isolation. Ensure your partner(s) are aware of the benefits of 'engrossed' work.
- Some educational articles give impractical advice.
- You can never fulfil all of your teaching obligations.
- Drafting a plan for your next working day is vital, as it frees up your mind for the benefits of downtime.
- It is counter-productive to push teachers, or push yourself, to work extremely long hours. The human and financial costs are high.
- Downtime is essential to recharge your energy and thus become a more effective teacher.
- Do not be drawn into doing any work in the evenings or weekends, no matter how small. When you're done, be done.

5. <u>Lesson planning</u>

Planning your lessons meticulously must be at the forefront of your priorities as a teacher. Teaching great lessons and ensuring that students consistently make progress and learn in your subject are the core foundations of your role, and therefore lesson planning cannot be neglected.

It takes me approximately one to two hours to fully plan a single period lesson, sometimes more. You might be thinking, 'I can't afford to spend that much time on lesson planning!'. Let me tell you something: you can't afford NOT to.

The first and most obvious reason is that, as mentioned previously, if your teaching is exceptional, everything else that comes with the profession comes together. It determines the fate of your career. All of your (numerous) other obligations are ancillary, and must not take control of your valuable working time. The only way to excel at teaching is to plan thoroughly, given that it enhances your own subject knowledge and boosts your confidence. Excellent lessons lead to engaged students, sustained progress over time, high attainment, less need for intervention and behaviour management, and time rewards for you in the long run.

The aim is not to spend the whole time lesson planning. The aim is to plan once, but do it so well that you reap the benefits long afterwards. For the first two or three years of my career, I spent a significant amount of time planning my Key Stage 4 lessons. That was 15 years ago, and I still use those lessons now. Needless to say, I have tweaked, adapted and modified features continuously over the years, but the fundamental structure has remained the same. The fine-tuning takes minutes. The time I invested all those years ago creating high quality resources has not only enabled me to teach great lessons, but has also saved me hours of planning in subsequent academic years. And I've been able to share the materials with colleagues who have used them too.

Imagine what your life as a teacher would be like if it took you just thirty minutes to an hour on a Friday to plan all of your lessons for the following week. That's pretty much how long it takes me.

The other – perhaps not so obvious – benefit to comprehensive lesson planning is that it's a skill which you develop over time. The more time you devote to planning your lessons, the more you stretch your abilities, becoming more efficient at it – both in terms of how long it takes you to produce the desired resources, and in increased quality of content. This is enormously beneficial when, for example, a new specification or course is introduced. And let's face it, things in education change ALL the time.

Plan what to plan

So, let's delve into the nuts and bolts of lesson planning. First and foremost, you must be astute about what you are going to be planning. You must *plan* what to plan. The reasoning behind it is that, depending on what stage you are at in your career, it may not be possible to plan every single lesson as thoroughly as you would wish, because of time restrictions.

Start with examination year groups, as these provide the most immediate and visible returns to the time you put in, and work your way backwards.

Another important aspect is considering prospective changes. You MUST think long-term – the longer the number of years you can use these resources for, the better. Are the lessons you are planning for a course that is being discontinued? Are you planning mainly chemistry lessons, when you'll be required to teach physics next year? Are you planning Key Stage 3 lessons when the following year, you'll only teach Key Stage 4 and 5? If you answered yes to any of these questions, start elsewhere. Reflect on your personal circumstances first, and only then embark on your preparation.

You are now ready to start planning your lessons. From my experience, there are two effective approaches you can take. The first one, which I detail below, is my preferred one.

Textbooks

Start with a book. This might sound archaic, but the best way to produce high-quality resources for a lesson is to begin with a course textbook. Courses created by the big educational publishing companies come with good textbooks, teachers' guides, lesson plans, schemes of work, assessment packs, revision resources, digital materials, etc. These are created by authors who are specialists in your subject, many of whom are or were teachers themselves. They also had the time you now don't have. The bulk of the work has been done for you, so all you have to do is optimise what is already there and adjust it to your teaching style.

I'm always perplexed when I came across colleagues creating resources from scratch – out of thin air – expending so much time and energy trying to come up with something bespoke, which ends up being lower quality than what you can generate from a worthy textbook and course; things that were downright ignored. If tailored resources and lessons is the goal, a book should still be the outset. It will provide you with lesson objectives and outcomes; task ideas (including differentiated ones); starter and plenary activities; personal learning and thinking skills; interleaved content; co-construction guidance; retrieval tasks; group, pair and independent work; key terminology; assessment for learning suggestions; literacy and numeracy support; cross-curricular links; homework recommendations; social, moral, cultural and spiritual maps; and probably all of the other elements your school wants you to include in your lessons. Books offer much more than what you can come up with on your own. Save yourself some time and brain power for the actual lesson delivery. There is no need whatsoever to reinvent the wheel.

Having said that, please bear in mind I don't just go into my lessons and get the students to open a textbook on a certain page and ask them to get on with it. I don't have whole class sets of books. To plan my own lessons, I look at a certain unit and the corresponding teacher's guide pages. I consider what needs to be taught and how I am going to teach it. I look at the sequencing of the suggested tasks and adjust them appropriately to my teaching style, as well as my students. I improve what is in front of me. I then create a visually engaging PowerPoint presentation which allows for pace to be significantly increased (for instance, content and answers come up with a click). Once I've finished producing the high-quality presentation, I make a copy of it and name it 'student handout'. I remove all the answers and add lines for students to be able to write on. Then I print it, two slides per page, and give it to the students. Most of the classwork is completed on the handout, while the exercise book is used for extension/challenge tasks and extended writing. That's it. Nothing flamboyant. Having a handout prevents all the 'dead' time copying things from the board, which adds little in terms of progress. It also allows students who were absent to quickly catch up on what they missed. Ever get the student receptionist come in mid-lesson asking for work for that student who's in the isolation room? No problem, just give them the handout.

Eventually you will have whole module handouts – as is the case for me. This also saves significant amounts of photocopying time, as you only have to do it once for a large number of lessons, as opposed to every lesson. At the end of teaching a whole unit of work, students are left with a revision resource, which is another added benefit. An additional time-saving aspect is the avoidance of handling glue. My finicky traits made it very clear to me after a couple of years of teaching that glue could not be a feature in my classroom – I'm sure that as a teacher you're aware of the aftermath of handing a glue stick to a teenager, so I won't go into detail (that's a whole other book!).

This whole lesson planning strategy might have left you somewhat bemused. PowerPoint? Textbooks? Please note that there isn't a requirement for you to be constantly seeking the next big thing or frequently changing the type of activities you do. You are not a Silicon Valley startup. Once you find what works for you and your students, stick to it. I dip in and out of about 10 to 12 activities for all my lessons, and with this approach my students continually make progress and achieve excellent examination results – consistently above national averages and regularly in the top 10%.

It's important to understand that resources are assistance elements to your lessons. Whether the lesson is fantastic or not is down to you, with the support of the materials you produced to go with it. A brilliant lesson comes from your passion, energy, enthusiasm, excitement, dynamism, eagerness, and the positive learning-based relationships you've formed. It doesn't come solely from the brilliant worksheet or power point presentation. Having said that, when planning lessons and preparing resources, aim for perfection. Perfection is impossible, but if you aim for it, you will achieve excellence.

Other teachers' resources
While a course textbook is my preferred method to follow when lesson planning, as well as the most beneficial in my view, there are other equally effective approaches you can take. There is an argument that if you make your own resources, these will likely directly translate into better lessons, since you know precisely how those resources support the progress and the learning of the young people in front of you. There are also teachers who are not fond of using lessons and resources made by others. Nevertheless, if used correctly, other teachers' materials can present some advantages too, which I outline below.

The most obvious benefit is that it can save you some time. As mentioned earlier, you may have to prioritise which lessons to plan. Examination year groups come first, with other classes following closely behind. Utilising someone else's resources potentially allows you to get lessons planned quicker, without compromising on quality.

An additional benefit to seeing or using materials created by other teachers is that it can help enhance your own resources and planning. You can get into someone else's mind and see things from a completely different viewpoint. You might consider mechanisms you hadn't thought of before. It expands your personal resource-creating tools.

The first port of call should be your departmental colleagues. I'm aware that some co-workers are not keen to part with the resources and lessons that they put time into preparing. That's their prerogative, and I respect it. However, many more are willing to share, as in my case. I'm mindful that in passing on what I have created to others, I'm able not only to have a positive impact on those I directly teach, but also to make a much wider contribution to the school and its students. It gives me a sense of satisfaction and accomplishment and makes my work feel appreciated. Side note: I have always shared my resources, not just when I became a Head of Department.

Many schools have centralised folders and areas where department's resources can be placed and easily accessed by team members. Through this, collaborative work is also encouraged, even if it's a simple discussion about a certain lesson or topic. It positively affects not only the teacher on the receiving end, but also the colleague who shared their expertise and materials.

A further point to consider is that you may be producing something that already exists. That excellent worksheet you have just dedicated an hour to creating? Sam has an identical one – and he's happy to share. The quiz with exam style questions you produced this morning? Anne made a very similar one last year, and it's available in the shared area. A small amount of research can save you a significant amount of time.

Important: Do not merely pick up resources created by other teachers to use in your lessons. You MUST adapt, adjust, modify and make them your own, so they become compatible with your own teaching methods.

Nowadays, you don't even have to be restricted to your most immediate colleagues. As we saw in a previous chapter, technology is a double-edged sword, but there are some good lessons and resources online, if you know where to look.

There are many teaching websites available, but the most useful platforms to locate resources created by other education professionals are the Times Educational Supplement (TES) and Teachers Pay Teachers (TpT). These offer a vast amount of materials of all kinds, which can be worth looking into if you're strapped for time or if reaching out to others in your team didn't yield results.

How to find adequate resources is whole different matter, but for the same reasons as above. An abundance of resources does not mean a profusion of quality. Start by typing as many key words as possible into your search, as these will likely harvest the closest results to what you're looking for. If nothing is found, remove the least significant word or phrase and search again. Keep doing this until the findings are worth looking into. It's unlikely that you'll have just a couple of items to scrutinise, so again you must continue carefully to make it an efficient use of your time. If the resource is free, simply download and assess it. If it is paid, read the description as it can give you a valuable insight. Not only will it give you an inkling of its suitability, but also of its quality. If the author took the time and effort to write a thorough description, then the actual resource is likely to match it.

If you're still not convinced, look for ratings and reviews. There are two main reasons which direct someone to leave a review – if the product is poor and they feel deceived, or if it's excellent and they want to show appreciation for its quality (though the former is much more probable). If someone took the time to appraise it, they've done some of the work for you in terms of deciding if it is worthwhile purchasing it.

One note of caution: if you're going to look for resources online, you must first quantify how long it takes to find them. The fact that there's so much out there can be a hindrance just as easily as it can be a help. If it takes you longer than 15 minutes to find something of quality, you are probably better off creating it yourself, as it will most likely be quicker. Remember that if/when you do find what you are looking for, you will still have to adapt, adjust, modify and make it your own.

Important: NEVER pay for online resources out of your own pocket. This book is about making you more effective at mastering your workload, not about making you poorer in the process. Schools spend millions of pounds every year buying resources from big companies, so buying resources created by another teacher should not be any different. Ask your line manager to purchase it from the departmental budget. If you need something straight away and can't wait to speak to someone first, make sure you get a receipt and later claim expenses. You are purchasing these resources because they will ultimately help your students to progress. However, if you are told that the school is not willing to pay for them (which would be incomprehensible), then do not buy them at all.

Key takeaways

- Planning lessons thoroughly is your number one priority.
- If you plan thoroughly on one occasion, you will reap the benefits for numerous subsequent academic years.
- The more you plan, the more you develop lesson planning skills, becoming better at it and producing higher-level content in a shorter amount of time.
- You must plan what lessons you are going to be planning.
- Course textbooks are the most effective starting point to plan a lesson, as they provide the most comprehensive guidance.

- Create 'perfect' visually appealing resources with a student handout.
- Handouts have several benefits, such as increasing the pace of a lesson, as well as providing students with a revision source.
- You don't have to change the type of tasks you do all the time. Once you've found what's effective for your teaching, stick to it.
- Lesson resources are supporting elements to your lessons. The true value provided comes from you.
- Using other teachers' resources can also be useful, as it can save you time and help you develop your own lesson planning tools.
- If not creating your own materials, check out resources from other colleagues in your department first.
- If looking for resources online, measure how long it takes you to find something suitable.
- Look for detailed descriptions, user ratings and reviews of paid products.
- Do not pay for resources out of your own money.
- When using materials created by someone else make them your own – adapt, adjust and improve.

6. <u>Marking and feedback</u>

Marking: the bane of every teacher's life. The Department for Education's Teachers' Standard 6 ("Make accurate and productive use of assessment") states in its fourth bullet point that teachers should "give pupils **regular** feedback, both orally and through accurate marking, and encourage pupils to respond to the feedback". On the other hand, Ofsted recently affirmed that they "do not expect to see any specific **frequency**, type or volume of marking and feedback". Contradictory? Absolutely. Marking is a minefield for every teacher and every school.

This leads to teachers spending on average three to four hours a week marking. Roughly 18% of us devote seven or more hours a week to giving students written feedback, while some mark for as long as fifteen hours (this was me a few years ago). That is the equivalent of nearly two extra workdays per week. This is completely unsustainable, and all it leads to is burnout and animosity towards the profession. Feedback, particularly written feedback, has therefore made it into this book because it can be more effective, and also because there are colossal opportunities to save time.

Let me make something clear: giving feedback to pupils is vital for learning, written marking is not. Most feedback is verbal – it does not need evidencing with a stamp – and is something you do naturally and frequently in any case. Written feedback is also a method to move students forward in their learning journeys and has its own benefits, the main one being that students receive personalised comments on their work, which may not always be possible to give to a whole class verbally. The two methods go hand in hand, with oral feedback taking the lead.

Writing comments on pupils' work should never be something you do because someone is 'looking over your shoulder', to pass a work scrutiny or an Ofsted inspection. This is a futile motive, which is not only time consuming but also adds little to no value to learning. I'm hopeful that the most recent Ofsted framework will give school leaders and teachers clear guidance on feedback since it states that "teachers check learners' understanding systematically, identify misconceptions accurately and provide clear, direct feedback". This sounds quite straightforward and encouraging to me and corresponds to what I have been doing effectively for a few years now.

The fact that I changed my own marking practice arose from a need. At the time that the job took its toll and my mental health was affected, I had a Head of Department teaching timetable with 11 classes, from Year 7 all the way to Year 13. I taught 210 students, which, even if it took just 5 minutes per exercise book, equated to 17.5 hours of marking. To meet the fortnightly expectation, I would have to give students written feedback for about nine hours a week. In reality, A level marking alone took me the whole of Saturday, and sometimes part of Sunday, so those figures are conservative. These circumstances added to a standard teacher's workload led me to a difficult decision: carry on and put my life on hold for the next thirty-something years (and dig myself an early grave in the process), leave teaching and find a new career, or become more effective. I chose the latter. If you find yourself in a similar situation, rest assured that what now works for me will work for you.

As we have seen, spoken feedback is paramount, with written feedback used for the sole purpose of complementing it. In the interests of clarity, all the strategies I'm about to lay out relate to written feedback, which is where there is more scope for enhancing efficiency and saving time. There is a place for it in teaching, and the reality is that you are always going to have to do some, as schools are not ready to dismiss it altogether just yet.

Peer and self-assessment

First and foremost, everything and anything that can be marked by students – both self and peer-assessed – should be marked by students. You must always ask yourself whether what you are about to mark could be done by a student or a non-specialist teacher without difficulty if they were given a mark scheme. If the answer is yes, then you should not be marking it yourself. This applies to classwork, homework and even summative assessments. Not only does allowing students to regularly mark their own work save you time, but it also leads to additional progress. It gives students an opportunity to reflect on their learning, identify individual misconceptions and, in turn, give themselves their own feedback – this is invaluable and not something you can even come close to matching when you mark everything yourself. Save your hard-won expertise for the deeper tasks such as an essay or extended answer, which will return more value for the time spent on it.

'But Bruno, if I get students to mark most of their work themselves, I'll be wasting a lot of learning time!'. Quite the opposite: allowing students to check, reflect and mark their own work is part of learning, not a separate element that you do in isolation.

I mentioned that I used to spend the whole Saturday and part of Sunday marking A level work, especially homework. It was so time-consuming that it affected my relationships with family and friends. And the most exasperating part was that the pupils hardly even looked at it. It had an insignificant impact on their learning and progress. Approximately 80% of that same marking is now done by the students themselves in lessons with my support. I mark the other 20%, but sometimes that too can be accomplished in lessons. The shift is evident. Pupils are empowered, and they ask questions about their errors, which leads to healthy discussions and overall improvement at a faster rate.

Important: Do not mark a piece of work which can be self- or peer-assessed just because 'it won't take long'. This attitude, combined with your workload, is what leads to an unmanageable work-life balance.

Marking exercise books

Giving written feedback in students' exercise books is undoubtedly the most challenging component of marking. Psychologically, it's difficult to look at a hefty pile of books and feel eager to get started. The task seems like a mountain to climb, so it gets put off time and time again. Do you ever take a set of books home only for it to come back to school untouched? Do you find yourself counting how many books you have left after each one you mark? Do you avoid certain tasks in lessons because they will result in more marking? This is not at all uncommon in the teaching profession. However, there are alternatives to the time-consuming nature of marking exercise books, both in terms of making it more effective as well as less demanding on your time.

Before you even open a book and give some written feedback, do some maths. This is to tackle the 'I can't face it' feeling that immediately comes to mind when you look at the stack in front of you. Let's say you have 28 Year 8 exercise books you want to mark before their next lesson and that today is Monday with the next lesson being Wednesday. Divide twenty-eight by three (Monday, Tuesday and Wednesday). All you now have to do is mark nine books on each of those days. Looking at nine books to mark is, mentally, a much smaller hurdle to overcome than looking at the full pile of 28. You can mark nine books in no time and feel a sense of accomplishment. Marking 28 books in one go would take much longer, and that's if you even have the determination to start it in the first place. They key is to break it down into smaller manageable chunks; just ensure that you keep marked books separate from books you've yet to mark, to avoid wasting time checking if they have been done or not.

You're now ready to mark, but you're only going provide written feedback where it's required. You will most likely know what that means before you start marking so simply stick to it. Choose quality over quantity as spending hours writing pages' long pieces of feedback doesn't directly correlate to enhanced student progress. Less is certainly more when it comes to writing comments in books. When you do write, make sure that it's meaningful and allows students to advance. Avoid 'fake' marking at all costs, even if you're worried that you're not writing enough, and that it might not bode well in the upcoming work scrutiny. I can assure you it will be fine; your priority is to support students in their learning, not to pass the quality assurance process with flying colours. The quality of your marking, and teaching, will rise to the top. You don't need to engage in superfluous games.

If it's time to mark that set of books, but you're not marking something specific, that's fine. The same strategies as above apply – don't write for the sake of writing. The strategies I'm about set out can also apply when you aren't marking something specific.

What you're going to do is skim read the classwork that students have carried out. Flick through the pages (no ticking) starting from where you last left off and keep reading. You are "checking learners' understanding systematically". At some point you will find errors, so in effect you have "identified misconceptions accurately" – don't write anything just yet, but keep a mental note. Keep reading until you reach the last page with classwork on it. On this page, "provide clear, direct feedback", which students can action, based on the misconceptions you spotted.

Notice the "clear, direct feedback" in the Ofsted criteria wording. Let's look into it further, and devise what to actually write. The vast majority of schools expect to see a WWW (what went well), an EBI (even better if), and a NYM (now you must) or Next Steps / Action – whatever your school calls it.

Simply eliminate writing a comment for WWWs and EBIs. What students have done well was… what you required them to do! If tasks were accomplished successfully, it gives you the evidence your teaching of that specific topic was effective. WWWs do not warrant personalised written comments; sometimes it might even be a challenge to find something positive to write about (sad, but true), and you spend a lot of time stating the obvious or you write something shallow. Nonetheless, successful completion of classwork will not go unnoticed. Make a quick note – mental or otherwise – to give general positive feedback on what you were impressed with to the whole class, when you ask them to look through the marking and complete their actions. If something particularly outstanding caught your eye, feel free to mention those students by name, as this will go a long way.

As far as EBI's are concerned, the same rules as above apply. Simply eliminate writing a personalised comment and instead give the whole class a verbal judgement of what did not go as well as intended and how it could be improved. You are, in effect, retrieving a topic and… teaching! An additional motive not to write a personalised EBI (apart from saving you time) is that it is too similar to the Next Steps, NYM or Action. You end up writing the same thing in other words, which takes up valuable brain power just trying to come up with something slightly different to say, for no added benefit. Needless to say that, in the case of EBIs, no students should be singled out in front of the class.

By removing the need for a written comment on what students have done fittingly and what can be perfected, and replacing it with verbal feedback instead, you have saved yourself hours of marking time as well as brain faculties. You have not, however, compromised on the quality of your feedback.

One important element of marking students' classwork which certainly merits a personalised comment is the Action. This is where, on the last page of completed work or where you have marked something specific, you give penned feedback. This MUST address the misconceptions you identified when reading through the work. It must be clear – students should be able to understand the instruction plainly without you having to explain it any further. This piece of writing is what will move the student forward in their learning, hence its significance and benefit. When you hand the books back to students, allow them adequate time to accomplish their differentiated tasks independently.

The last, but not least, step is to fold the corner of the page where you finished off your marking. The next time you pick up that book, you'll carry on straight from the point where you left off. This not only saves you precious minutes when opening it, but also allows you to check if the previous action was completed successfully, without having to look for it. Just remember to make sure that you let students know why you've folded the page corner and ask them to leave it that way.

If your school requires teachers to use stickers with WWWs, EBIs and NYMs, my best advice is, quite frankly, not to use them. Firstly, over the course of the academic year, it adds up to hours of just sticking them into exercise books, not to mention the exasperating feeling when you run out, and then have to engage in a school-wide sticker treasure hunt. Asking students to stick them into their books themselves is not an option either; this is not an appropriate use of learning time and quite a few of those stickers would end up sideways or upside down on the page, no matter how many times you demonstrate the correct technique.

The other main issue with having a marking sticker is that it coerces you into writing something which may be completely unnecessary. As we've seen above, WWWs and EBIs do not necessarily warrant a customised written comment, as this takes up valuable time, not only when writing them but also in thinking about what to write. Verbal feedback is as effective and much less time-consuming. Having a partly blank sticker looks poor, so simply eliminate this ineffective tool. The quality of your verbal and written feedback is what adds value to student's learning, not the sticker.

Marking assessments and mock exams

When it comes to marking assessments, there's no option but to put pen to paper. However, some of the tips presented above can certainly be used or adjusted when grading exams.

To begin with, remember that anything which can be marked by the students themselves should be done in this way. A good example are questions which require a multiple choice or specific answer. These can easily be marked by the students with a clearly displayed mark scheme on the board. Peer-assessment works better than self-assessment when it comes to formal tests, since it avoids the temptation for the student to be generous when marking their own work.

Once you've got your students to mark everything that can be carried out with their help, it's time to correct the remaining more challenging assessment questions. Start off by checking what students have marked themselves. The vast majority will be correctly graded, however in the interest of reliable results, you must look through it. This will take a fraction of the time it would have taken you to mark those papers yourself. You are just confirming the accuracy of the students' input.

In order to mark the rest of the assessment, do some maths again, just like what you now do when marking exercise books. The biggest difference is that you're not going to split the task into smaller numbers of whole papers. You are going to divide the questions themselves. Suppose you have three papers to mark, which equates to twenty-one questions altogether since you've already eliminated the bits and pieces that students have corrected. The deadline for completion and entering the data is in seven working days' time. Divide 21 by 7. The task at hand is now practicable and the target is clear: mark 3 questions per working day. Add this to your daily plan, and you're good to go.

The advantage of splitting exam marking into questions (and not whole papers) is that if you mark the same question consecutively, you become extremely efficient at it. After you've marked a few, you won't even need a mark scheme, substantially reducing the overall length it takes you to achieve your goal.

Marking homework

Checking students' completion and quality of homework is another feature of marking that deserves a plan to increase time efficiency as well as providing quality feedback to the students.

First and foremost, all of the strategies portrayed above work very well when it comes to work completed outside of lessons: peer and self-assessment, splitting the task into small manageable chunks and only giving written feedback if it truly warrants it i.e. moves the student forward.

Depending on your subject, you may see your students as little as once a week or as much as six times. You really have to decide whether you can afford to use lesson time to mark, in this instance, what students have done for homework. Unlike work completed in exercise books, homework tends to focus on tasks taught in class to increase the speed of learning, demonstrate mastery, review work, study for tests, and retain specific skills over time. I would advise you not to use lesson time, but that's entirely up to you as it depends on your own subject circumstances. In my opinion, most homework doesn't require written feedback, so I recommend that you don't provide it. Most of the homework I set falls under one of three categories: worksheets, website-based homework, or revision homework.

Worksheets can be used to consolidate knowledge of a learned topic or to prepare for the next lesson. This is my most used method for homework, and it may well be yours too. I haven't marked one in writing for over ten years even though I assign them weekly or fortnightly, and yet it remains an extremely effective way to allow students to make progress. All I do is collect the homework and then skim read each piece; I identify the main misconceptions and which students completed exceptional work, as well as those who struggled or clearly did not put expected effort in – a quick jot down on a sticky note does the job. As I read each piece, I log the quality of the homework on a tracking sheet with the grading of 1 to 4 (one being the highest, and four meaning not completed). This spreadsheet is conditionally formatted so that the cell automatically changes colour between green, amber and red as I enter the number, and is fairly straightforward to put together even if you dislike spreadsheets – if you'd like a blank template, email me at bruno@teacherworkload.com as I am happy to share. Using numbers also allows for an average to be calculated easily.

Over time, I have a document of evidence regarding pupils' homework completion and quality and no matter how large the class is, marking and logging a homework task using this approach never takes longer than fifteen minutes. The feedback I give to students is then verbal, which uses up approximately five minutes at the end of a lesson. I display the spreadsheet on the board after I've told students my findings, as this encourages healthy competition and discussion. Side note: students get very excited seeing all the pretty colours on the board next to their names, no matter how old they are, hence why I wait until the end of the lesson. Displaying the spreadsheet also has an additional benefit: students ask if they can improve a certain homework or complete ones for which they were absent. This may be because they want to achieve more in their work, 'surpass' a peer, or simply because they're aware that I'll be showing this tracking document at parents' evening. Their reasoning is irrelevant: it makes the homework more effective and it has an overall higher positive impact on students' progress and my teaching. By using this strategy, you'll once again be slashing the amount of time it takes you to mark something without compromising on the quality of your feedback. In turn, you'll also be making your teaching practice more effective.

Website-based homework can also be effective and save you time. As we saw in a previous chapter, technology can be a double-edged sword. If used correctly, it can boost learning, but if used incorrectly, it can hinder progress and be a source of infinite distraction. There's a vast array of educational websites available for you to choose from that can support you with homework (and classwork) and save you considerable amounts of time. You must first analyse whether the electronic resource truly allows students to increase their knowledge – is it effective? – or if it's just another diversion. If it fails this test, eliminate it from your homework setting tools. From my experience, websites which use algorithms to adapt and personalise students' education to their abilities, prior knowledge, and performance work best.

Once you've come across a worthy internet-based instructional source, another important point to consider is whether it will do your marking for you. Not only must it lead to customised progress, but it should also grade and analyse students work, and make all of that data available to you.

For example, I use Memrise as a vocabulary learning website and application. Even though it's specifically used to learn foreign languages, I got the idea from a science teacher who had been using it for a few years. I've now shared the way I use it with other colleagues, and I'm aware that other subjects use it too, so it is worth looking into, no matter what your specialism is. It allows me to create my own courses and direct students to learn exactly what I want them to. It then gives me statistics, such as study time, words learned, words healthy in long term memory, difficult words and course progression for EACH STUDENT. I put in the work once (to create the course) and in return I receive an everlasting resource, which provides me with invaluable information, with no added effort. You might not even have to create the initial course yourself, as there are a considerable number already available. You just need to ask students to join and then monitor it. Side note: in order to track personalised progress you must create a group. Once this is done, you'll be given a link which students must click on, allowing you to track their studies.

Seneca Learning is another web-based educational platform which is worth looking into. It claims to allow students to learn faster and memorise better as it applies cognitive neuroscience to make learning more efficient and enjoyable. It uses spaced repetition, active retrieval, interleaving, multimodal representations, and visual memory cues to increase students' retention of information. Once again, it can be a useful homework tool due not only to its effectiveness, but also because it presents the teacher with individual tracking information, covering learning time, average scores, sessions completed, and correct answers. Another advantage with this online platform is that it offers over 250 free courses covering all subjects and exam boards, so you don't have to create anything yourself in the first place.

The two examples named above are the two main online resources I use effectively for homework in my practice. They may or may not work for you. Do your research, and see if you can find other electronic tools which match the effectiveness and tracking criteria for your subject – removing the need for you to mark.

Revision homework is the final category of homework I use often. No, not simply telling students to go and revise for an upcoming assessment or exam. Directing students on what to revise and how is key here, as is obtaining the evidence that this has been accomplished. There are plenty of revision techniques, but only a couple are in fact effective. These are the ones you want to stick to, as they'll return more worth for any given amount of time spent on them. Remember that we want to make everything in our teaching, including homework, effective, but we also want to ensure that it doesn't take up large amounts of time with a requirement for written feedback.

From my experience, the most valuable revision homework is something which allows the student to test their own knowledge, as this has been identified as boosting performance, particularly if applied over a distributed length of time. Simply ask students to create a mind map or flashcards on a given topic.

This has multiple benefits: it provides you with the evidence that students have revised what you asked them to with no need for written marking and, more importantly, it fosters practice 'tests' which require recall from memory. Students can simply test themselves or a peer and create two piles of flashcards – if they correctly remember an answer, they can pull the card from the stack, and if not, it goes back into the 'to learn' pile. Students should also be encouraged to get the answers right on more than one occasion by returning to the deck of flashcards another day. If they're resilient until they remember each concept correctly, they'll increase their chances of recalling it during an actual exam.

Marking and feedback lessons

All of the marking and written feedback strategies specified above will undoubtedly make you more efficient, with the added advantage of rendering your teaching practice more effective. These alone, when incorporated consistently into your daily plan, may be sufficient for you to obtain a well-deserved work-life balance. However, there are times during the academic year when a teacher's workload simply becomes engulfing, no matter how productive and organised you are. If you are using all of these strategies to keep up with your written marking, but at times still find yourself having to extend your daily cut-off point, or take exercise books or assessments home, then it's time for one final powerful strategy: marking and feedback lessons.

In a previous personal example, I mentioned that in a certain academic year I taught the full range of secondary school year groups, which equated to 210 students. The expectation regarding written marking in addition to standard Head of Department obligations made sticking to the marking policy, frankly, unattainable. As a result, I introduced marking lessons throughout the academic year. If you find yourself in a similar situation, I would suggest that you do too.

Decide on what lesson(s) and year group(s) you will be using to conduct your written feedback, as well as what you will be focusing on, whether it's classwork conducted in exercise books or an assessment. Once you have determined these elements, plan a series of activities which students can carry out INDEPENDENTLY. The classwork and instructions you set during such lessons must be effortlessly understood by the students, in order to avoid interruptions to your marking flow. Although the classwork must be engaging, don't spend too long planning what to give to students, as this would render the strategy counter-productive.

For example, around Halloween, Year 7 classes watch *Coco*, an animated film based around the Mexican Day of the Dead holiday. We play it in Spanish with English subtitles, so that it's not only both topical and cultural, but it also allows for language learning. As they watch it, students complete a worksheet about the film. This is not exclusive to my own classes – I've added it to the Schemes of Learning so that everyone in the department benefits from it too. The only requirement for these lessons is that they are used solely for written marking, not other work. Side note: yes, you've read that right. I stick a film on for students to watch while I mark their work. If there are films in your subject which are educational, topical and promote student progress, why shouldn't you use them in lessons?

Explain to students that you'll be coming around to each one of them and giving them written – as well as verbal – views on their work. I understand that you may not be able to mark a whole class set of exercise books or assessments in one or two lessons, but you will certainly make a sizeable dent in the task at hand. Then, there'll only a handful of marking left, which can simply be added to your daily plan.

You may well be thinking at this point that there's no way some of your classes will 'engage' in independent learning without going off task. You must trial it and see. If it works with some classes, but not with others that's okay. Stick to the ones where this strategy is effective, and you will at least be able to reduce your written feedback obligations to an extent, even if not fully.

When I introduced marking lessons to my own teaching practice, the only goal was to keep up with the demands of written feedback, but I exposed an additional noteworthy benefit. It allows for one-to-one conversations, which never seem to happen in a standard 'frantic' lesson. You really do end up giving personalised feedback to students, as discussions naturally lead to queries and answers, and misconceptions are addressed more deeply.

Important: Don't be tempted to accomplish other work during these lessons. This time should be set aside solely for

the written marking of classwork or assessments of the group
of students you have in front of you.

Key takeaways

- Ambiguous guidelines from official educational bodies has
  led to unsustainable expectations for written marking.
- Feedback is essential for effective teaching, but it does not
  have to be provided exclusively in writing.
- Penned feedback must always have student progress in
  mind, not a work scrutiny or someone checking up on you.
- There are several strategies which can reduce the amount
  of time you spend giving written feedback, while retaining
  (if not increasing) its effectiveness.
- Everything that can be peer- or self-assessed should be,
  even if marking it yourself would 'not take long'.
- Allowing students to mark their own work provides
  opportunities for self-reflection, which in turn leads to
  enhanced progress.
- When marking classwork in exercise books, divide the
  whole set into small manageable chunks. Mark only a small
  number of books a day.
- Steer clear of time-wasting 'fake marking'. Write only
  meaningful feedback which moves the student forward.
- Read through students' work and write comments on the
  misconceptions you identify on the last page of completed
  work. They must be clear and concise.
- Give verbal feedback regarding WWWs and EBIs. Save the
  written feedback for the NYM, Action, or Next Steps,
  which has a higher impact on individual student progress.

- Fold the corner of the page where you last marked an exercise book.
- Do not use written marking stickers. They are time-consuming and a hindrance.
- Assessment questions that can be marked by students should be. Peer-assessment is more effective, but be sure to double-check what students have graded.
- Divide the task by the number of questions rather than the total number of papers. Mark a certain number of questions until you hit the deadline.
- It's up to you whether you use lesson time to mark homework or not, as it depends on your subject circumstances.
- All of the strategies apply equally to marking homework, although it is less likely to require written feedback.
- When setting a homework worksheet, read through students' work and log its completion and quality on a conditionally formatted spreadsheet.
- Websites which use algorithms to adapt and personalise students' education to their abilities are an effective homework method. Ensure that websites or apps also provide you with data on student completion and performance.
- Ask students to design a mind map or create flashcards for revision. These are most effective and provide you with evidence that students have revised.
- If all written marking strategies still do not allow you to keep up with your workload and achieve a work-life balance, introduce marking lessons.

- Give students meaningful and engaging independent classwork to complete (an educational film is appropriate). Speak individually to each student and give written feedback, as well as verbal.
- Marking lessons have a double benefit: they create time where you would otherwise be engaged, and allow for deeper one-to-one discussions.
- Do not use marking lessons to do any other schoolwork.

7. **Behaviour management**

Yes, it's behaviour management again. There are a ton of studies, books, reports and articles on successful behaviour management of students. So why dedicate a chapter to it? The truth of the matter is, despite all of the (excellent) literature available, managing student behaviour is still a significant cause of anxiety among teachers. About 70% of us report experiencing disruptive behaviour from pupils in their lessons weekly or even more frequently, with low-level disruption such as chatting and leaving seats without permission being among the most common grievances. Poor learner behaviour also ranks third in the aspects of the profession that teachers most dislike – right after workload and unnecessary paperwork – with 43% of education professionals attributing symptoms of stress at work to student behavioural issues.

And if teachers are experiencing it, then they will also have to 'waste' valuable time dealing with it. This means that teaching and learning in the classroom is less effective than desired, which in turn can add to the workload outside of the classroom, further inhibiting your chances of genuinely securing a healthy work-life balance.

The specifics of behaviour management are not within the remit of this book. I'm therefore going to keep this discussion focused on the topic of saving time when managing student behaviour, which directly links to the overall aim of this book. Even if it's not immediately apparent, the strategies presented below will help you to move closer to the ultimate goal: getting your life back.

First and foremost, there is NO such thing as behaviour management on its own. Knowing the behaviour policy inside-out and having a vast array of tools at your disposal is somewhat futile if it's not linked to effective teaching and positive learning-based relationships. A successful combination of these components is key.

Positive learning-based relationships

True account

Chloe is an Assistant Headteacher who is new to the school. Only a couple of weeks into September, everyone in the school already knows who she is – both staff and students. She is EVERYWHERE. You see her on the fields talking to students at break, in the canteen at lunch and at the front gate chatting to parents at the end of the school day. Throughout the day, you can hear her in the corridors constantly reminding pupils of expectations, and visiting classrooms to find out how learning is going. Already, students actively seek her out for support with various matters as she's gained their trust. Chloe is lively, spirited and dynamic. She uses humour in a positive way to promote well-being and to help build positive relationships. I was astonished both by how quickly she became 'part of the furniture' and by the impact it had on relationships: students who could be considered challenging already pretty much do as they're told when she addresses them.

What did Chloe have that I didn't? Have you ever had a Head of Year walk into your lesson and have students immediately become focused, sit still, stop fidgeting and listen intently? What does that Head of Year have that you don't (yet)? The answer is a strong learning-based bond with both students and their parents. Pupils are aware of who they are and accept them as someone in authority. This has come into place through being 'visible', communicating effectively, and engaging with the young people under their care all the time.

A good learning-based relationship with students is paramount in teaching. Students will work for YOU, the person who stands in front of them day in and day out. As a teacher, you must establish and build a base of trust, which doesn't just happen automatically. This is particularly important if you have just started your career or are new to a school, as some students find it difficult to trust new teachers and will, in turn, play up in lessons.

Be visible

Whether you've been at the school for a while or have just started in the new academic year, the most powerful way to start building relationships, or strengthen existing ones, is to be visible and let students know who you are.

There are a few ways in which you can boost your profile within the school without having to stand in the corridors introducing yourself to every pupil. The most effective way is to lead an assembly for each year group. You'll have the attention of the whole school. Assemblies are usually delivered by members of the leadership team or Heads of Year, which immediately gives a sense to students that these are important people. If you put yourself forward and stand in front of a year group, you'll benefit from the same effect: 'this is someone important that I should respect'. Make the assembly interesting and link the theme to you in some way, showing your audience that you're human.

When I started at a new school in Nottinghamshire, the languages team and I led an assembly throughout a whole week on the topic of the European Day of Languages. The day falls at the end of September, so it was an ideal way to get my face recognised early in the academic year, and an opportunity to tell students a bit about myself. I told students about my language learning journey, the fact that I'm not a native English speaker, and that I speak six languages. Sharing this information acted as a catalyst for several subsequent conversations. During that same week, I stood at the front gate at the end of the school day, which allowed students to come up to me and find out more about me as a person, or tell me about their own language learning experiences. It was an effortless way to build relationships with both students I taught and those I didn't.

At my previous school, every member of staff got a 'free' lunch, on the condition that they had it with students in the canteen. This was an astute way to foster relationships outside of the classroom, as well as providing passive supervision. Other effective methods to raise your profile within the school, and create opportunities for informal conversations with students, are the staff pantomime, the end of year video cameo role, or the sports day staff relay. Yes, get training now!

I advise you to be proactive and take a leadership approach. Lead an assembly, or any other whole school event, and then create opportunities to engage with students about it – whether by standing at the front gate or simply having lunch in the canteen with pupils. It will directly correlate with fewer initial incidents of misbehaviour in your classroom, and less of your valuable time spent dealing with it.

…and invisible

As we've just seen, being visible is key to building relationships and reducing the need to manage student behaviour. It's important to note that all of the strategies presented above have one common feature: you are in control. You're leading the assembly when everyone is quiet and listening; there are plenty of other members of staff around at the front gate at the end of the school day; someone is on duty in the canteen at lunchtime. The 'control' you have in these circumstances makes it unlikely you will come across bad behaviour or have to spend time handling it.

But being 'invisible' may also be exactly what you need in order to reduce your workload. This may go against what you have, at some point, read in a book about behaviour management by an educational expert. It may go against what the leadership team constantly tell you. But if you're reading this book, it's probably because all else has failed, and you need a more drastic approach. Your well-being justifies it.

If every time you step into a corridor you end up having to deal with a behaviour related incident and its aftermath, don't step into that corridor in the first place. If you're not there to witness it, then you don't have to manage it. Out of sight, out of mind. You don't have to see the untucked shirts, the top buttons not done up, the coats inside the building, the trainers, the mobile phones, the headphones, the headlocks, the screaming, the swearing, the one-way system not being followed, the arguments, the missile throwing, the ripping down of displays, the pushing, shoving, tripping, crushing and running, the littering, the snogging, the fighting, the lateness, the truanting, the backchatting, the defiance, the rudeness, etc. etc. etc.

You don't have any control of the above. Avoid the hot spots and you're eliminating the time you have to spend dealing with corridor behaviour incidents, not to mention reducing your own stress levels. This strategy also applies to paid duties which you've volunteered to do. Calculate how much you get paid, including time spent afterwards dealing with whatever behaviour occurrences you came across. It is probably not worth it; your time is more valuable. So, again, eliminate it.

Needless to say, it's impossible to avoid the corridors and therefore incidents outside of the classroom at all times. Due to the nature of secondary schools, where teenagers are confined for a large part of their day, at some point you will have to manage misbehaviour incidents. In the first few years of my career, I spent half of my time planning lessons and the other half following up on behaviour disturbances. I was like a 'dog with a bone', where even the slightest mishap warranted a lecture, an email to the Head of Year, a behaviour incident log, looking through student photos to find out names of culprits, and so on and so forth.

Looking back, this approach was the wrong one. You can handle most corridor behaviour occurrences with a firm "off you go!" or a quick word, ideally by pulling students aside, away from an audience. Job done. You're not ignoring the misdeed, but you're not going to make it an integral part of your workload either.

An ounce of prevention is better than a pound of cure

As mentioned in a previous chapter, planning your lessons thoroughly is the foundation of effective teaching. Without question, the best tool to deal with misbehaviour is preventing it from ever happening in the first place. This is why giving your lesson planning due care and attention is paramount. Remember, it's something you can't afford NOT to do. Rigorous planning leads to inherently higher levels of confidence. Lessons must be interesting, engaging, and matched to students' needs and abilities, as well as ensuring success. They should be 'pitched' to the top, with plenty of extension and challenge tasks, but delivered in a way that those less able can also access content and continue to make progress.

As well as lesson planning, there are other important elements to consider before you even start a lesson, which will also play a part in avoiding misbehaviour. This is where organisational skills come in, as these will eliminate any 'dead' lesson time and, therefore, opportunities to go off task. Plan the logistical aspects of the lesson and ensure that you have all the materials ready and available for learning to begin as soon as students walk into the classroom. Some examples include:

- Logging into the computer beforehand and opening all the digital resources you'll need for your lessons that day. If you teach in different classrooms, go to each one of them in the morning and ensure this is done. Although this might seem like a waste of time, moving from one classroom to another makes it likely you'll get there at the same time as the pupils, so at least your digital resources will be ready to go.

- As well as electronic materials, it's also vital that all physical resources are fully ready and available. Lay out exercise books, worksheets, glues, highlighters, mini-whiteboards or anything else that's needed in the lesson. Ensure you have whiteboard pens and board rubbers in good working condition. If you don't teach in the same classroom, again make sure you go there in the morning and leave the necessary materials. Valuable lesson time should not be used to fluster around looking for resources. If you're using a PowerPoint presentation, invest in a 'clicker', which allows you to circulate the classroom. Side note: do not teach from behind the desk.

- Have a 'teaching first aid' kit ready. This should include pens, lined paper, and a box of tissue. I understand that students coming to class without the right equipment is a major bugbear for teachers, but for the sake of your sanity and the learning of the rest of the class – who have everything they need – don't enter into a discussion with students about any of these items. 'Why don't you have a pen?'; 'You've forgotten your book again!'; 'You just had break, get some tissue in your own time'. The truth of the matter is that we may not always be aware of a student's personal circumstances. They may not even have been given breakfast that morning, so a pen is the least of their worries. You'll have to provide them with the equipment at some point anyway, so just do it immediately. Otherwise, you're just distracting the attention of the other students, for whom the discussion is not relevant.

- Don't ask students to line up. As soon as students start arriving, get them in and keep telling what task they are to get on with immediately. Lining up outside the classroom can block corridors and it's an opportunity for pushing, shoving, poking, prodding, jabbing, nudging, tapping and the lot; in other words, incidents that you will then have to deal with before any learning has even occurred.

- 'The bell went two minutes ago; time for another activity.' Wrong. End your lessons in plenty of time. Time management proficiency will ensure that not only does your lesson ends purposefully, but – more importantly – the following one starts smoothly. Stop whatever students are doing five minutes before the end of the lesson, even if they're in the middle of something, and ask them to pack away. Students should be standing behind their chairs with all resources put away two minutes before the official end of the lesson. If your school doesn't have a bell, dismiss students just before the end. If there is a bell system, dismiss students on the dot. Allowing students to go on time gives you precious minutes to either move to your next classroom or to ensure everything is set up before your next class arrives. Side note: dismiss students in rows or small groups in a steady manner, to avoid a crush, or more mindless physical contact.

During lessons

As stated above, the details of behaviour management are not within the scope of this book. However, there are some key strategies which are worth considering when it comes to reducing the time spent dealing with misbehaviour and – consequently –reducing your workload.

Starter tasks

The best tool at your disposal when it comes to lessons running smoothly is to do away with any opportunities to go off task. Always have a starter/entrance/immediate task ready for when students come into your lesson. This should not be as simple as 'write the date and title'. It should be something relevant, but which does NOT require teacher instructions. In other words, a task that can be carried out straight away by conscientious students, while you focus on settling in those who need some extra support. It doesn't have to be something new and exciting every time. In fact, the more students are used to a certain type of starter activity, the more likely they are to engage with it instantly when they arrive.

Clear instructions

Ensure that all of your instructions are meticulous and precise. I cannot emphasise this point enough. If there is one common oversight regarding behaviour management that I've encountered throughout my career, it is unquestionably regarding the quality of instructions. If students understand what they are required to do, they are very likely to do so. It is as simple as that.

Before you give an instruction, ensure that everyone is quiet, sitting still and facing the front or you. If you're not happy that this is the case say: '*your back needs to be touching the back of the chair*'. Don't start talking until you have absolute silence and are confident students are listening to you. This is a key step, which is often bypassed because of concerns that lesson time will be wasted if you don't just 'get on with it'. This leads to all sorts of problems further down the line and over the course of an academic year. Students get used to getting away with not listening and bad habits that become much harder to break once they're embedded.

Once everyone is attentive (no matter how long it took to get there), you're ready to tell students what you would like them to do. You can do so yourself with plenty of pauses and 'student-friendly' terms, as well as visual aids to keep your audience in check, or alternatively you can give students some silent time to work out what they have to do and then ask a volunteer to explain it the rest of the class. The latter is my preferred technique, since it encourages an active approach to the task we're about to embark on, rather than a passive one.

Regardless of which method you use, you must then clarify the command and ensure that students are fully aware of the requirements of the task. Explain it yourself if you asked a student to do so initially and vice versa. Then ask one or two pupils to repeat to you what they must do, particularly those who you know need more support (you are, in effect, differentiating to match their needs).

The final step is to model an example of the activity that you're setting. Even though care has been taken to explain, consolidate and check, some students might still not realise what to do. Seeing an example usually dissipates any doubts that are still left. At this point I usually say something along the lines of: *'if you're not sure what to do, please let me know. It's simply because I didn't explain it well enough, so I need to do better'*. This gives students a sense of confidence to put their hand up and ask. It helps them overcome that anxiety that it is their fault if they haven't understood the instruction.

A clear sign that an instruction was successful is that ALL students will be immediately on task. If there is fidgeting, restlessness, or low-level chatter, I'm afraid to say that the commands weren't clear enough and you must start again. Provided that the classwork matches students' abilities, this shouldn't happen.

Make effective use of the countdown

This is another behaviour tool that I've seen wrongly employed repeatedly in my role as a mentor or Head of Department. 'Three, two, one' said tentatively in under two seconds, and no change in student behaviour ensues. There are times where you need to regain the attention of the class, so you should do so in a confident manner. Start counting down from five in a firm tone of voice with a pause in between each number. As you are doing so, tell students after each number what you would like them to do, what you can see is happening, or what action you will be taking. Here's an example:

"5 – YOU NEED TO BE QUIET…
4 – YOU NEED TO LISTEN…
3 – YOU NEED TO BE FACING THE FRONT…
2 – Show me your listening skills…
1 – Most people are ready…
Zero."

The volume of your voice decreases at the same rate as the noise in the classroom, becoming more mellow as students quiet down and follow your instructions. This approach works in the vast majority of cases in getting a whole group of students to focus on their work or you. It must not, however, be overused. In other words, if you're having to do a countdown every five minutes, then there are other underlying behavioural issues that you need to address, such as lesson planning or learning-based relationships.

For those especially challenging classes, or for extreme poor behaviour circumstances, the countdown can be adjusted in order to match the difficulties you're faced with. The main difference is that when you get to zero, you will act and apply a sanction to those who didn't follow your instructions. You will, of course, let students know what will be happening. For instance:

"5 – YOU NEED TO BE QUIET…
4 – YOU NEED TO LISTEN…
3 – YOU NEED TO BE FACING THE FRONT…

2 – WHEN I GET TO ZERO, I WILL ISSUE A (mention your school's behaviour policy, e.g. C1, negative point, warning)…

1 – Most people are ready…

Zero."

At this point, you must follow through with a sanction immediately if anyone is still not attentive. If, as you're doing so, the remaining few students quiet down, do not continue issuing sanctions. Students have in effect done what you've asked them to do, even if not immediately. Feel free to acknowledge this and remind students that those who had not yet followed instructions at zero, but were not given a punishment must do so in future. You have high expectations, and you won't let anything get in the way of learning. They may not be so 'lucky' next time.

Important: Don't allow yourself to enter into a discussion about who else should have been given a negative sanction at zero, even if students say it's unfair. The only unfair aspect of this whole process is the fact that learning is being disrupted.

Effective praise

The final, but by no means least important, in-lesson strategy is the use of effective praise. You're probably sick and tired of hearing about the 'catch them being good' cliché. Well, you've heard about it for good reason: it works. "Positive point", "house point", "merit", "well done", "Vivo", "excellent effort", and other positive behaviour reinforcement phrases should be rolling off your tongue constantly in lessons. It promotes a favourable learning atmosphere, provides students with the kind of positive reinforcement that builds on success, motivates them to learn, and increases their participation in class. Effective praise is sincere and focuses on effort, resilience and hard work. This doesn't mean, however, that it should be given for trivial accomplishments, weak efforts or innate intelligence.

As a reminder of this behaviour management aspect, each of my classes has a positive behaviour chart. It's simply a class list printed on card with a row of tick boxes in front of each student's name. Every lesson someone is assigned the role of monitor – which everyone loves doing – and ticks names when I give a positive reward. This happens pretty much every time a pupil displays effort and takes part in the lesson, whether well or not so well. It reminds me to keep praising with the added benefit of compiling a 'student participation' graph. A quick glance tells me who the big contributors to the lesson are, but also – more importantly – who might be 'hiding' or not being targeted enough with questions.

Detentions
All of the strategies presented above will, for the most part, prevent incidents of poor behaviour. There are, however, occasions where further action is required, and this is where a detention may be issued. The fact of the matter is, in its standard form (sitting for 30 minutes to an hour staring into space) a detention is an ineffective sanction and an ineffective use of everyone's time, especially yours. It's clearly not a powerful enough deterrent, or you wouldn't see the same faces over and over again scattered throughout the school at the end of the day

– or even worse, sat in the lunch hall in a mass detention completely detached from the cause of the problem.

Imparting this kind of punishment can, in itself, be an unearthly process: the dreaded 'you have a detention' exchange, and the ensuing backlash; making a note of it in the student's planner, which has magically been misplaced; logging it on the system only to find out the perpetrator has a busy detention schedule and is not available for the next few working days. Even if all these steps are successful, you then have to hope that the student attends, just so that you don't have to engage in the immense follow-up process. In the meantime, several days have passed and there's been no meaningful closure. The root of the issue must be addressed with higher positive-impact tools, using as little of your time resources as possible.

- First and foremost, talk to the student about the misdemeanour as soon as possible. This should ideally be straight after the lesson. Use that minute of spare time you have after dismissing the class, or break/lunch if it happens to be that time of day. This should be a short, to the point conversation, about the negative impact that the poor behaviour is having on the student's learning, as well as the learning of others in the class. Explain to the student what you would like to see instead. This is a vital step, as the pupil may well not know how to behave.

- If there's no breakthrough in subsequent lessons, have the restorative conversation once more. Ensure that the student is aware that you won't allow learning to be disrupted, and that you will take further action in order to see an improvement in future lessons. You don't have to go into detail about what these actions might look like.

- Get as many people 'in the loop' as you can. Let Heads of Year, Tutors and members of the leadership team know that this student is making poor choices regarding their behaviour and this is negatively affecting their learning. Colleagues will, in turn, strengthen the message that subpar behaviour will not be tolerated. **Important:** do not just pass the buck to someone else. You're simply making other members of staff aware of your concerns. The main bulk of measures to tackle the issues must come from you. This is empowering.

- Call the student's parents and inform them of the behavioural issues you're encountering in the classroom – don't let the students know you will be calling home. Make sure you keep the conversation focused on the topic of learning and how it's being negatively affected by the behaviour. Remember that you are talking about someone's everything, so any personal criticism is likely to be faced with an adverse defensive reaction. Explain what support you've put in place and how you must work together to overcome the difficulties, as well as what you would like to see happen and the positive impact this will have. Finish the discussion by agreeing to a follow-up phone call in a few weeks' time.

- Make the aforementioned follow-up phone call. The vast majority of students, if not all, will have improved by this stage and met your high expectations, so all you have to do is let their parents know. If this isn't the case, the next step is to arrange a parental meeting with all parties involved. If possible, ask the Head of Year to be present as well. This will be a serious dialogue about expectations, and how unsatisfactory behaviour is gravely affecting the student's learning as well as your teaching. Parents will be further informed if the issue is not successfully addressed and further action will be taken. The message is that the pupil's education is paramount, and that it will not be jeopardised, certainly not under your watch. This is non-negotiable.

Key takeaways

- Managing student behaviour is still a significant cause of apprehension among teachers; it also takes up a considerable amount of time.
- Successful behaviour management is a combination of positive learning-based relationships, effective teaching and knowledge of a range of tools to handle poor conduct.
- Strong learning-based relationships are paramount in teaching – students will work for YOU.
- Make yourself 'visible'. Increase your profile around the school. Lead an assembly, talk to students at the gate at the end of the school day, or take part in whole school events.
- …and 'invisible'. Eliminate instances of misbehaviour that are out of your control, such as poor corridor behaviour. If

you came across it, deal with it there and then, with a stern word away from an audience.

- Rigorous lesson planning prevents most unsatisfactory conduct from happening in the first place.

- Ensure logistical aspects of the lesson are also looked after – this should include digital and physical resources, letting students into the classroom straight away at the start, and ending lessons in plenty of time.

- Always have an effective starter activity ready that does not require teacher instructions.

- Make certain that all instructions are meticulous and precise. Only speak when everyone is listening, clarify the command, and model an example of what you would like students to do.

- Make effective use of the countdown. You should tell students what to do after each number with a firm tone of voice and a pause in-between.

- Praise students constantly for their efforts in order to promote a positive 'knock on effect' on learning.

- Detentions detached from the cause of poor behaviour are ineffective and take up a considerable amount of your precious time.

- Have restorative conversations with students as soon as possible after poor conduct occurs.

- Let as many colleagues as possible know about your concerns. However, do not just 'pass the buck'.

- Call parents and inform them of the current poor behaviour choices and the negative impact on learning. Work together in order to achieve a positive outcome for the student.

- If all the previous strategies are unsuccessful, arrange a parental meeting. This must be a serious encounter where expectations regarding learning are clearly laid out, as well as plans for further action that will be taken if there is no improvement.

8. Other obligations

Interventions

Google 'Year 11 intervention' and you will find a fair amount of debate about whether 'interventions' and revision sessions work. Most significantly, however, you will obtain endless results of schools' revision sessions and intervention timetables. Nearly the whole of the Year 11 academic year is an onslaught of extra lessons, before, during, and after school as well as throughout the holidays leading up to GCSE exams – all of which puts considerable pressure on both students and teachers. Having to give up your limited time to offer revision sessions is another cause of an unmanageable workload. Let's delve into whether this type of 'intervention' is worth putting in place, and if so, how we can make it more effective.

It must be considered that, if you teach a Year 11 class, your main (most likely) Performance Management target is something like "achieve GCSE results in line with student benchmark targets". Performance-related pay was brought in to raise standards and outcomes for pupils, as well as to inspire teachers' development. The reality is that, when someone's salary is at stake in a field like education which has so many variables – not to mention hormonal teenagers – the focus simply becomes the grades that group of students achieves or doesn't achieve. Everyone else, Year 10 downwards, is put on the back burner. This leads to the mad scrap you witness at schools, where revision sessions are added at any available time, students are taken out of regular timetabled lessons to sit in a whole day 'intervention', and then make up for missed lessons with more 'intervention' days, cramming in as much 'revision' as possible. 'Blanket' sessions are counter-productive and must not be part of your plan to raise attainment. They also send out the message that if a student doesn't work hard in lessons, something else will be put in place for them.

Although some would argue that you shouldn't provide any revision sessions at all, the reality is not that straightforward. There is a place for giving up a productive amount of your time, as long as this is targeted at those who truly need it. The main goal, however, is not necessarily to offer extra sessions, but instead to reach a point where these are not required, due to the precursory work you have put in. Most 'intervention' must happen in lessons, where you have the bulk of time with students. This should be plenty to ensure that most pupils, if not all of them, achieve grades in line with their perceived abilities. Let's 'intervene':

- First and foremost, focus on your lessons. It takes me back to the importance of lesson planning which, I reiterate, determines the fate of your career. This could not be more accurate than when we are talking about a GCSE class in the final academic year of their courses. Focus on teaching great lessons throughout, and you will have most likely reduced the need to provide any extra support in those last few months, when those students are being pulled in every direction. Consistently excellent lessons will lead to good attainment. End of.

- Instil a sense of responsibility in your students. Last academic year, I was asked by a student if I would be putting on any revision sessions after school or during the holidays. I replied there would be two every week, Mondays and Fridays period 3, when we had our timetabled lessons. There would also be several other sessions each week, including weekends and holidays, which would be led by herself. Ensure your pupils are aware that what they do in lessons is what has the most impact on their academic success, or lack thereof. Revision sessions are, for the most part, to be conducted independently – they do not replace timetabled lessons.

- Ensure that students are doing everything you ask them to do. As well as teaching great lessons, concentrate your efforts on making sure this happens outside of the classroom too. Set effective and meaningful revision homework weekly – remember that you must direct students on what to revise and how, as well as obtaining evidence that this has been accomplished. As mentioned in a previous chapter, flashcards or mind maps work best, since these allow students to test their own knowledge. Once set, ensure you follow up with those who haven't completed their homework, as this means they haven't revised for their upcoming examination. Speak to parents regularly and inform colleagues, such as Heads of Year and Tutors. The more people that are spreading your message to those specific pupils, the more likely it is they end up doing what you need them to.

- Identify the main underachievers. The strategies stated above apply to the general cohort, but you will need to pinpoint where underperformance is the case so that you can take appropriate action. This is where a robust set of data on student performance is essential. A few years ago, all you needed to know was who was below a C grade, and that was who got targeted. Nowadays, prior high attainers are as much at risk of underperforming as those with a perceived lower ability. If we're talking specifically about Year 11, a mock exam is the most accurate method to determine who is furthest away from the desired target grade. Once the mock tests have been marked, it's time to analyse the results. I use a detailed tracking spreadsheet which provides me with information on how individual students have performed on each of the four Modern Foreign Languages papers, an overall grade, and how the latter compares to their target. All I then do is sort the list of students from those furthest away from target grade to those on or above 'holy grail', and those at the top get earmarked for 'intervention'. I'm lucky enough to be married to a Data Manager who has created awesome, automated, simple but extremely effective spreadsheets that I can use effortlessly for my own classes. If marrying a Data Manager is not an option for you, worry not. I have mock exam tracking spreadsheets for most GCSE subjects (and a video tutorial), and I'm happy to share them with you. Just email me at bruno@teacherworkload.com with the subject you require. In return, all I ask for are your thoughts on this book. Just a few lines will do, as any feedback is appreciated!

• Once you've analysed your mock exam results, share these with your classes. Put the results up on the board and discuss what went well and where there's room for improvement. Share your 'intervention' plan with the students i.e. what you expect from them in and outside of lessons. Change your seating plan and place those who need that extra boost at the front, closer to you. This way you can instinctively target them with more questions in lessons, and instantly check the quality of their classwork, providing immediate verbal feedback – you are 'intervening'. In the last few weeks leading up to the exam, I go as far as completing most written classwork on mini-whiteboards, or even directly on desks – students love it and baby wipes rubs it all off – so feedback is constant and on the spot, since time is of the essence.

- Despite all your best practice, you may want to – or have to, for the sake of the dreaded Performance Related Pay targets – put extra sessions in place for those who are at risk of doing less well than expected. This could be simply because you started at a new school, and the class you inherited had a lower starting point than desired, or you were given a Year 11 group that previously had a variety of teachers and less than ideal teaching and learning, among other reasons. If you decide to give away your time, this must be carried out in a methodical and planned way. First, only those students that your tracking has identified as underachieving should be 'invited'. This list should include those below their target grade, but not necessarily all of them. There will some pupils on this list where extenuating circumstances simply prevented them from performing to the best of their ability (e.g. non-attendance due to illness) and you have other evidence that this will not be case come the actual exam. With these students out of the list, now look at those who you are certain won't work to the best of their capacity (they need a lot of prompting in class) and can be disruptive to learning. This will be a very small number of students, but asking them to attend will be counter-productive. If you're going to make the extra sessions effective, it is indispensable that they truly are targeted – hit-and-miss targeting does not work. You're now left with a small group of students to whom an extra lesson or revision session really can make a difference. Arrange this for a time that suits you – I suggest you ask for one or more mornings of tutor time (some schools do this anyway) where you would be otherwise engaged. Morning sessions are substantially more productive, as you will know from teaching that Year 8 class period 1 on a Tuesday and period 5 on a Friday – it's like they're a different species. Once again, let parents and colleagues know that you've put this intervention in place. This is where your input stops. If students choose not to attend, don't use any more of your time following it up or offering it at another time. Apart from a mention in the following lesson, the onus is on the pupil and their parents – otherwise you're falling just short of sitting the exam for them.

Important: Revision and extra lessons should not be used to make up for insufficient curriculum time. The time you have been given for standard timetabled lessons should be plenty to achieve desired outcomes. If it's not, there's a bigger issue that must be looked into. Extra sessions are, as I set out above, targeted to the small minority of pupils whom you have identified as below target and in need of extra support. If you choose to offer a revision session on a weekend or during a holiday, make sure that this is paid. Otherwise, do NOT do it.

Extra-curricular activities

"One fifth of the planet speaks Chinese". "Mandarin Chinese is the mother tongue of over 873 million people, making it the most widely spoken first language in the world". "China is one of largest trading partners of the United Kingdom". "Knowing Chinese may give students an edge when competing for an important position". "China will play a major role in world affairs in the future; as China now has opened up to the West, there are opportunities for employment in all areas".

These are just some of the statements that I included in a letter to parents when I introduced the Mandarin Chinese enrichment programme at a school where I worked for seven years. When I started working there, the school set aside periods 4 and 5 every Friday for this enrichment purpose. It was fantastic for me and my students. I planned and delivered Mandarin lessons where there was no pressure to achieve results, no unnecessary paperwork, no constant data snapshots – just good old-fashioned teaching which led to high levels of student enjoyment, progress, and achievement. However, students didn't just leave with a solid knowledge of beginners' Mandarin. I entered them for an HSK Level 1 test, which is the most recognised Chinese language qualification in the world. At the end of the academic year, I took pupils to the London Confucius Institute at the School of Oriental and African Studies, University of London (SOAS). For four years in a row, every single student passed and obtained the qualification. I considered this to be a great achievement for the students, myself and the school. In the fifth year, the school ended the timetabled enrichment programme. I'm unsure of the reasoning behind it, but I would guess it was related to budget pressures. I continued offering the lessons to students as an after-school club for the following two academic years.

Other opportunities I've offered to students include a variety of educational trips. For over ten years I organised Key Stage 3 day trips to France, Key Stage 4 residential trips to Barcelona during the Easter holiday, and a Key Stage 5 week-long work experience in Madrid during February half-term. As you are well aware, putting together such extra-curricular activities is exceptionally time-consuming, not to mention that myself and other members of staff would give up part of their holidays to attend. Side note: I was told one of the school's governors insisted these trips happened during the holidays. I never had a chance to speak to this governor and ask if his employer expected him to work for the benefit of his company outside of normal working hours – unpaid. That would have been, no doubt, an interesting conversation.

The benefits for the students are, nevertheless, enormous: improved relationships between staff and students, an extended and enhanced curriculum and learning, providing a balance to the pressures of the classroom, expanding students' horizons, developing new skills and increasing in students' resilience, self-confidence and well-being, to name but a few.

I don't currently offer any of these activities in addition to the normal course of study. When my personal well-being became affected by my workload, in addition to meticulously applying the strategies previously mentioned in this book, I had to make the very difficult decision to eliminate these extra-curricular pursuits from my regular work. This decision was a source of great conflict. On the one hand, I want to provide my pupils with as many opportunities as possible, but on the other, I have to keep my sanity.

According to analysis of official data by the Trades Union Congress, the average teacher works 12.1 hours unpaid every week. That amounts to 9 million hours of free labour each week, or 462 million hours each year.

You may find yourself in similar circumstances. You're reading this book because you'd like to achieve a healthy work-life balance and manage your workload effectively. You're left with two options:

Eliminate any activities that you lead: clubs, productions, concerts, trips, teams. Unless your contract specifically requires it, you offer these voluntarily. If they are 'imposed' on you, be very clear about saying no, and very vague about the reasons why – state personal reasons.

Ask for a time budget. Mention to your line manager what you'd like to offer as an extra-curricular activity, as well as the benefits for the students, and request some protected time in your timetable in order to plan it. "But Bruno, my school will never give me a 'free' period to conduct the school's Drama production". Well, if you ask for nothing, you get nothing.

One thing is certain: providing students with a variety of out-of-hours activities, and the unquestionable benefits they bring, must not be run on free labour and teachers' goodwill, and absolutely not at the expense of our mental health and well-being. If our political leaders keep shrinking school budgets, they may well end up with just exam factories. On their heads be it.

(Unnecessary) paperwork

It's 6:00pm on a Saturday evening, and I'm at the accident & emergency department at East Surrey Hospital with a loved one who is unwell. I'm in my third year as a qualified professional and I have a full teaching timetable from Year 7 all the way to Year 11. As we sit in the waiting room, I have my laptop with me, so I can get on with tackling the latest initiative. All teachers have been directed by a new member of the Senior Leadership Team to write a few notes in a spreadsheet about each student they teach. We are told this won't take long, as we only have to write a few lines per pupil. Two to three minutes ought to do it. The reason behind it? *If* Ofsted come, it will show that we really know our students... Whenever I'm asked to do something 'in case Ofsted come' alarm bells start ringing in my head. I strongly believe that any duties should be carried out because they present clear benefits to the students, not solely for potential inspection purposes.

At the time, I taught roughly three hundred students, so that equated to a minimum of ten hours on top of my standard workload. Multiply that by the 80 teachers in the school and you could be looking at around 800 hours of typing information we already know into a spreadsheet.

This is called the 'some benefit' method, which is when only the benefits of engaging in a task are taken into consideration, and not its downsides. Unnecessary and duplicative paperwork is, unfortunately, rife in schools and it leads to high levels of frustration, stress, and loss of confidence for teachers, along with reduced performance in the classroom and an unsustainable workload.

I'm sure you can think of many occasions where this has happened to you. In the example above, the benefit could be that you reflected on each student you taught; the downside is that it revealed nothing new and this is something you do naturally daily – you just don't write it down. It took valuable time away from the actual work of educating and supporting our students, and the value of the reward is extremely low given the amount of time that needed to be spent on it. In the end, I didn't even finish it, as the workload took over and I simply forgot about it – no one ever asked to see it, not even Ofsted when they did come. Side note: they would have had to read thousands of annotations – 80 teachers x 1000 students.

Once again, it would be hypocritical to simply say "don't do it!". It's not that straightforward, especially if everyone else seems to (reluctantly) get on with it. However, I would certainly advise you to engage in constructive feedback and questioning. I've done that in all the schools I've worked at. From writing to the leadership team about behaviour systems and how these could be streamlined, to providing practicable alternatives in staff surveys for managing workload and increasing effectiveness. All of these contributions have always been well received. By working together with colleagues and school leaders, I've had a positive impact on the whole school. You can too.

If you're faced with what you feel is a burdensome initiative, ascertain its purpose – this should be clear, relevant to the intended audience, and in line with school values. The workload impact should be proportionate to the benefits it brings to the students. If it's not, ask for it to be eliminated or reduced. Other legitimate questions are: "How useful is it to pupils, teachers, senior leaders or parents?"; "Would we engage in this initiative if there was no Ofsted visit looming?"; "What would happen if we didn't ask teaching staff to do this?". The answers will give you a good indication of how worthwhile the task is. Any such tasks that you do have to do should be added to your daily plan, after your own priorities. You should then only spend time on them in proportion to the value they provide.

Important: You are not that difficult person that just moans about everything they're asked to do. As mentioned above, we must work together with senior leaders and colleagues to provide solutions, alternatives and constructive feedback for the benefit of staff and – ultimately – students.

Key takeaways

- 'Blanket' revision sessions or interventions are counter-productive.
- Interventions must be targeted at those who truly need it, and should mainly happen in lessons.

- Focus on planning and teaching excellent lessons – this will reduce the need for intervention in the first place.
- Instil a sense of responsibility in your students. Set meaningful homework and provide revision strategies. Follow up on non-completion with parents, tutors and Heads of Year.
- Clearly identify underachievers through robust assessment and tracking systems – feel free to ask for my GCSE tracking spreadsheets.
- Change seating plans and place students who are underperforming at the front, closer to you. Question them more often and provide further (verbal) feedback.
- If you need to provide extra sessions, ensure that it is solely for those who are underperforming, as hit-and-miss intervention is ineffective. Morning sessions are more productive.
- Revision sessions should not be used to make up for insufficient curriculum time.
- If you're asked to provide holiday revision lessons and decide to do so, make sure these are paid.
- Extra-curricular activities bring enormous benefits to students. They must not, however, be run on teachers' goodwill and free labour.
- In order to balance your workload and home life, you may have to make a difficult decision and eliminate any extra-curricular activities you offer. If your well-being is suffering, you must do so.
- Ask for a time budget. Request some protected time in your timetable in return for the time you put into offering extra-curricular projects.

- Real-term budget cuts have a negative impact on being able to offer a balanced school experience to our students.

- 'If Ofsted come' must not be the sole reason to ask teachers to carry out a task.

- The 'some benefit' method is rife in schools: meaningless tasks that only consider benefits (no matter how small) and not the much bigger downsides.

- The impact of engaging in such tasks is very high in terms of time spent. The returns are very low in terms of value added for students.

- Unnecessary paperwork takes away valuable time from the actual business of teaching our students. It reduces performance in the classroom.

- Work collaboratively with colleagues and senior leaders. Give constructive feedback, offer alternatives and ask the right questions. Don't just be that 'difficult' person.

- Add any such tasks to your daily plan after your main priorities. Time spent on them should be proportionate to the value they bring.

9. <u>Thank you</u>

Hi, I'm Bruno and I'm a Teacher of Modern Foreign Languages (Spanish, French, Portuguese, and Mandarin Chinese) in my fifteenth year as a qualified professional at the time of writing.

I'm originally from Portugal and come from a low-income family. My parents grew up under a 40-year dictatorship, which kept its people poor, illiterate and living in fear. Just to put it in context, the per capita income at the time was lower than in Nazi-occupied France, and the lowest in western Europe. Dad finished his education in Year 4 and mum made it to Year 6. Looking back now, I realise the sacrifices they made, but they never allowed them to be noticeable to my sister and I at the time. There was always food on the table and a roof over our heads, and they ensured that I was able to be the first member of the family to go to university. My successful career is down to them. No matter how difficult life and the teaching profession can sometimes be, it doesn't even come close to what they had to endure, so I'm extremely grateful to them.

Having grown up in a deprived area and everything else that came with it, I decided in 2002 to buy a plane ticket and try my luck in the United Kingdom. I wasn't willing to carry on working at McDonald's, call centres, in construction, ferry boat painting, removals or as a translator for wages that hardly made ends meet. Although, I should say that it never did me any harm to work and study at the same time, and it taught me a lot.

I ended up settling permanently in the UK and worked for a couple of years in an upmarket London hotel as a room service attendant. I saw plenty of celebrities and was crowned Employee of The Year in 2003. Despite the accolade, the best thing about the whole hotel experience was that, by a stroke of luck, I met someone who would introduce me to teaching, as well as becoming a lifelong friend. Katherine's dad was the Head of English as an Additional Language Service in East Sussex, and they were looking for a Teaching Assistant to work with Portuguese and Spanish speaking students in a variety of schools. I got the job and never looked back. A year later, I was proudly studying for my Postgraduate Certificate in Education at Sussex University.

I have worked mainly in South London in mixed state comprehensive schools, and recently moved up to Nottinghamshire. I've been a Head of Department for eight years now, and at my previous school I was also a Lead Practitioner for Middle Leaders. I currently line manage Performing and Visual Arts as well as Modern Foreign Languages.

I truly enjoy working in education, making a difference and inspiring students, as well as supporting other members of staff. Through my various roles I have mentored, coached and guided hundreds of teachers and middle leaders. Seeing them develop and succeed as professionals is extremely gratifying and is certainly one of the aspects of the job that I enjoy the most.

Similarly, I've been pleased with my examination results throughout the years which have been above national averages both in terms of attainment and progress, particularly because they directly translate into further future opportunities for the pupils I teach. Their successes and achievements are paramount. In 2015, the Good Schools Guide awarded me a certificate for 'Excellent performance by Girls taking AS Spanish at an English Comprehensive School'. In certain academic years, my GCSE results have been ranked in the top 1% and 3% nationally. A few years ago, I was invited to speak at a Schools, Students and Teachers network (SSAT) Teaching Conference and presented 'Modern Foreign Languages: A Blueprint for Success' to other colleagues from a range of subject areas around the country.

The hard work I put in has regularly been recognised by parents, students and colleagues alike. This also gives me a great sense of satisfaction in what I do daily, and motivates me a great deal.

For years my achievements in education came at the expense of my well-being and personal life. However, when I made the conscious decision to ensure that I had a healthy work-life balance and apply the strategies I have laid out in this book, my performance did not suffer. In fact, I'm now more effective, productive and efficient. I'm not advocating laziness, and I don't shy away from hard work. I have, however, put in place the tools to ensure that my output is focused and balanced without compromising on the value I add to students, colleagues and the school. You can do so too.

If you had to make changes in your life to improve the well-being of a loved one, you wouldn't even think twice. So, make changes happen for you – your choices, your time, and your life.

The hours you've spent reading this book mean a lot to me. Trusting me with your time is a heartfelt privilege, and I would like to thank you for it. I hope you've found *Teacher Workload* a valuable template to reclaim your life back. I hope it allows you to enjoy your job without having to postpone your life until the next holiday. If it has helped you in any way, it has served its purpose.

I appreciate your feedback, so please feel free to leave a review on Amazon. Also, if you think this book could be beneficial to other teachers, please spread the word with colleagues and on your social media.

As mentioned previously, I'm happy to share my effective GCSE tracking spreadsheets. And if there are any other ways that I can support you, please feel free to get in touch.

Thank you again, and I hope to hear from you soon.

Bruno
bruno@teacherworkload.com

10. <u>References</u>

1 – The root of the issue ✓
- https://neu.org.uk/media/3136/view

2 – The mindset ✓
- https://www.theguardian.com/education/2019/sep/18/25-of-teachers-in-england-work-more-than-60-hours-a-week-study
- https://www.tes.com/news/least-70-teachers-working-over-contracted-hours
- https://neu.org.uk/policy/teachers-workload
- https://www.nasuwt.org.uk/advice/pay-pensions/pay-scales/england-pay-scales.html
- https://www.teacherspensions.co.uk/employers/managing-members/contributions/calculating-contributions.aspx#targetText=Contribution%20rates,-As%20the%20rate&targetText=Since%20September%202019%2C%20the%20Employer,employee%20in%20the%20pay%20period.
- https://www.nasuwt.org.uk/advice/pay-pensions/pensions/england/teachers-pension-age-and-life-expectancy.html
- https://www.nhsinform.scot/illnesses-and-conditions/infections-and-poisoning/shingles#causes-of-shingles
- https://en.wikipedia.org/wiki/Parkinson%27s_law
- https://www.theguardian.com/education/2018/may/13/teacher-burnout-shortages-recruitment-problems-budget-cuts

- https://assets.publishing.service.gov.uk/government/uploads/system/uploads/attachment_data/file/832634/School_teachers_pay_and_conditions_2019.pdf
- https://assets.publishing.service.gov.uk/government/uploads/system/uploads/attachment_data/file/819314/Teacher_well-being_report_110719F.pdf
- https://www.educationsupport.org.uk/sites/default/files/resources/teacher_wellbeing_index_2018.pdf
- https://www.tes.com/news/uk-teachers-work-some-longest-hours-world
- www.hse.gov.uk/statistics/
- https://www.theguardian.com/education/2019/apr/16/fifth-of-teachers-plan-to-leave-profession-within-two-years

3 – Technology vs time ✓
- https://www.tigermobiles.com/blog/mobile-phone-usage-statistics/
- https://www.bbc.co.uk/news/education-46959295

4 – Your school day ✓
- https://www.sleepadvisor.org/benefits-of-waking-up-early/
- http://healthysleep.med.harvard.edu/healthy/science/what/sleep-patterns-rem-nrem
- https://www.psychologistworld.com/memory/zeigarnik-effect-interruptions-memory
- https://pdfs.semanticscholar.org/16e5/2874d2679b969279793b57d67ec68e111223.pdf?_ga=2.137055093.470588960.1571807267-1460061527.1571807267
- http://www.its.caltech.edu/~squartz/rightchoice.pdf

- https://m.signalvnoise.com/why-we-only-work-4-days-a-week-during-summer/
- https://www.history.com/this-day-in-history/ford-factory-workers-get-40-hour-week
- https://www.theguardian.com/money/shortcuts/2020/jan/06/finland-is-planning-a-four-day-week-is-this-the-secret-of-happiness
- https://www.tes.com/news/spending-supply-teachers-rises-ps13-billion
- https://www.researchgate.net/profile/Marc_Berman3/publication/23718837_The_Cognitive_Benefits_of_Interacting_With_Nature/links/5aa05093a6fdcc22e2ce21c5/The-Cognitive-Benefits-of-Interacting-With-Nature.pdf
- http://citeseerx.ist.psu.edu/viewdoc/download?doi=10.1.1.183.1776&rep=rep1&type=pdf
- https://www.youtube.com/watch?v=GjLan582Lgk   How the Balmoral Hotel Helped J.K. Rowling Finish the Deathly Hallows
- https://fitproessentials.com/the-4000-round-trip-ticket-to-tokyo/

5 – Lesson planning ✓
- www.tes.com
- www.tpt.com

6 – Marking and feedback ✓
- https://teachertapp.co.uk/often-teachers-required-mark-work/##targetText=We%20have%20been%20gradually%20learning,mark%20up%20to%2015%20hours!
- https://teachertapp.co.uk/marking-like-no-one-watching/

- https://www.tes.com/news/workload-tens-thousands-teachers-spend-more-11-hours-marking-every-week
- https://neu.org.uk/advice/workload-marking
- https://assets.publishing.service.gov.uk/government/uploads/system/uploads/attachment_data/file/665522/Teachers_standard_information.pdf
- https://www.gov.uk/government/publications/school-inspection-handbook-from-september-2015/ofsted-inspections-mythbusting
- https://www.tes.com/news/we-must-end-obsession-marking
- https://assets.publishing.service.gov.uk/government/uploads/system/uploads/attachment_data/file/801429/Education_inspection_framework.pdf
- https://keydifferences.com/difference-between-formative-and-summative-assessment.html
- https://www.memrise.com/
- https://memrise.helpshift.com/a/memrise-learn-a-new-language/?p=web&s=groups&f=how-do-i-create-a-group
- https://www.senecalearning.com/
- http://repository.stcloudstate.edu/cgi/viewcontent.cgi?article=1030&context=ed_etds
- https://www.bbc.co.uk/news/health-22565912
- https://www.aft.org/sites/default/files/periodicals/dunlosky.pdf
- https://en.wikipedia.org/wiki/Coco_(2017_film)

7 – Behaviour management ✓

- https://dera.ioe.ac.uk/11236/13/090515practicalapproachesen_Redacted.pdf

- https://www.teachertoolkit.co.uk/2018/06/30/behaviour-management-tips-2/
- https://www.telegraph.co.uk/education/educationnews/5154590/Teachers-waste-16-days-a-year-dealing-with-bad-behaviour.html
- https://assets.publishing.service.gov.uk/government/uploads/system/uploads/attachment_data/file/184078/DFE-RR218.pdf
- https://teachingbattleground.wordpress.com/2018/10/24/the-worst-behaviour-in-school-corridors/
- https://neu.org.uk/advice/behaviour-tips-trainee-teachers
- https://www.gov.uk/school-discipline-exclusions
- https://www.thoughtco.com/effective-praise-8161

8 – Other obligations ✓

- https://arbor-education.com/blog-6-steps-to-create-an-effective-interventions-strategy/
- https://www.york.ac.uk/media/iee/documents/Closing%20the%20Gap.pdf
- https://dera.ioe.ac.uk/326/1/An%20evaluation%20of%20National%20Strategy%20intervention%20programmes.pdf
- https://missdcoxblog.wordpress.com/2017/03/11/year-11-interventions-holiday-revision-sessions-the-alternatives/
- https://johntomsett.com/2014/02/15/this-much-i-know-about-why-we-should-stop-intervening-and-focus-upon-improving-the-quality-of-teaching/
- https://deputyjohn.wordpress.com/2014/02/15/the-blight-of-interventions/

- https://schoolsweek.co.uk/headteacher-scraps-mad-year-11-revision-classes-to-protect-pupil-mental-health/
- https://classteaching.wordpress.com/2017/02/26/what-to-do-with-year-11-revision/
- https://www.crimsoneducation.org/uk/blog/benefits-of-extracurricular-activities
- http://www.in2teaching.org.uk/hints-and-tips/View/962.aspx
- https://www.schooltours.co.uk/blog/residential-trips-for-school-groups-and-the-benefits.html
- https://www.tes.com/news/teachers-work-more-unpaid-overtime-anyone-else

9 – Thank you ✓

- https://www.nytimes.com/1970/07/28/archives/antonio-salazar-a-quiet-autocrat-who-held-power-in-portugal-for-40.html

Printed in Great Britain
by Amazon